A history of

HIGH SALVINGTON

BOOK FOUR

Angela Levy

Best Wishes
Angela Levy

Published for Angela Levy by Verité CM Ltd.

ISBN No: 978-1-910719-54-1

Print and production management by
Verité CM Ltd, Worthing, West Sussex BN12 4HJ. UK.

www.veritecm.com

ACKNOWLEDGEMENTS

Grateful thanks to

Jane Dore

Information Librarian at Worthing Library

and to my Worthing Library Volunteer colleagues

Eileen Colwell, Linda Kane, Catherine Steeden, Carol Sullivan

CONTENTS

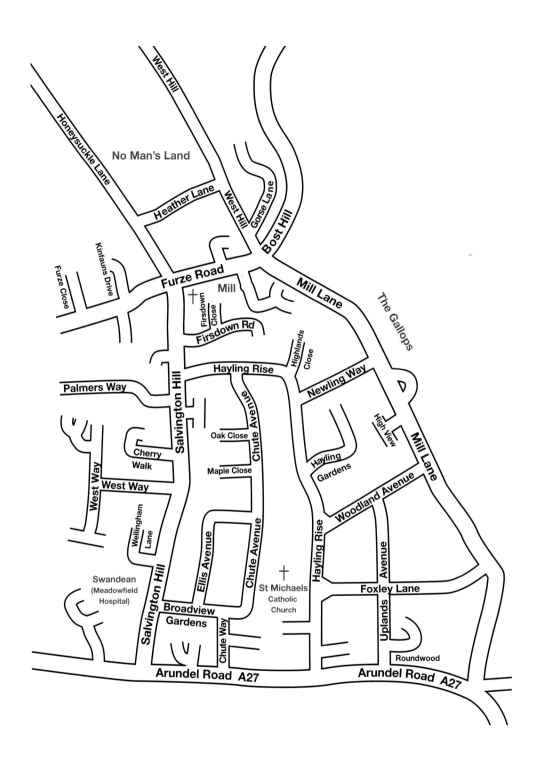

Map of High Salvington. Copyright the author.

CHAPTER ONE

BIOGRAPHIES

George Herbert Bloye OBE JP

George Herbert Bloye OBE JP.
Worthing Herald 14 February 1931.

George Herbert Bloye, known as Herbert, was born in September 1870 in Birmingham, the son of George Bloye, a plumber's brassfounder, and his wife, Mary, née Moore.

He was educated at King Edward Grammar School and went on to train for the Wesleyan Methodist ministry at Headingley College. From 1894 he travelled in Circuits in Somerset, Yorkshire, Birmingham and London as a Wesleyan minister. However, in 1910 he left the ministry on doctrinal grounds and wrote and lectured on social and political matters.

During the 1914-1918 war Herbert Bloye was Financial Secretary for the British Red Cross in Pall Mall and was awarded an OBE for his services.

After the war, he was Contributions Secretary at St. Bartholomew's Hospital and was made a Life-Governor in 1931.

Also in 1931, he was vice-president and president-elect of the Worthing branch of the League of Nations Union. At one time he was on the staff at their headquarters in London and represented Worthing on the national Council.

He was deeply interested in the Brotherhood and was its vice-president. He was president of the Labour Party in Worthing and travelled the county on their behalf.

Lecture notice. Worthing Gazette 25 May 1927.

He contested a seat in Selden Ward in the February 1931 by-election, supported by the Labour Party and trade unions. He was opposed by Mrs Millbank-Smith and G. W. Ayliffe. Herbert Bloye received 343 fewer than Mrs Millbank-Smith. In the same year he was made a magistrate.

His first wife, whom he married in July 1901, was Ethel Alice Moylan-Jones. They were divorced in about 1906 and it was not until December 1922 that he married again. His second wife was Martha Ada Pretoria Diss. There had been two daughters of the first marriage and there was another daughter of the second marriage.

When Herbert Bloye was made a magistrate in 1931 an article was printed in the Worthing Gazette which mentioned his acheivements and that he had recently been ill.

It was not this illness however, that was the reason for his death a few months later, however. He travelled daily to London and always cycled between Worthing Station and his home at 'Polrode', in Hayling Rise, High Salvington. He normally arrived home at about 7pm but on the evening of Friday 27 November 1931 his wife received the news that her husband had been involved in an accident.

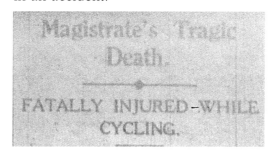

Accident notice. Worthing Gazette 2 December 1931.

It occurred in Warren Road about 200 yards west of the entrance to Worthing Golf Course. Leonard Pelling, a commercial traveller, accompanied by his wife, was returning home to Chichester when a car came round the bend with headlights fully on going in the opposite direction. Mr Pelling was temporarily blinded. He slowed from 20 mph to about 12 mph and dipped his lights but he knew he had hit something. The other car, presumably unaware there had been an accident, did not stop.

Mr. and Mrs. Pelling got out and found that they had hit the rear of Herbert Bloye's bicycle, not knowing that he was there. They laid him on the path, put a cushion under his head and stopped the next car that came along, sending the driver off for an ambulance.

A police ambulance arrived driven by PC Holder who noticed that the rear reflector of the bicycle was covered with mud, some of which was of long standing, making the reflector visible but not plainly so.

At the inquest, held at Worthing Hospital on Monday 30 November and presided over by the West Sussex Coroner, F. W. Butler, Dr. Henry Stuart Hamilton, Resident House Surgeon at the hospital, explained that Herbert Bloye had been unconscious on arrival and had never regained consciousness. He died just before 11pm as the result of a cerebral haemorrhage caused by a fracture at the base of his skull consistent with hitting his head on the road. There were no other injuries.

The Coroner praised the straightforward way that Leonard Pelling gave his evidence. However, he did suggest to the jury that Mr Pelling should not just have slowed down but should have stopped altogether.

The foreman of the jury, F. G. Searle, felt that it was impractical for drivers to stop every time they encountered an on-coming car with bright headlights.

After a short deliberation, the jury returned a verdict of Accidental Death and exonerated Leonard Pelling. They expressed sympathy to the widow. In addition, they wanted to urge cyclists to carry rear lamps and not only reflectors.

Tributes to George Herbert Bloye from J. Barnes, the Chairman of the Worthing Labour Party and C. A. Kerry, the Honorary Organising Secretary of the Brotherhood, were printed in the Worthing Gazette.

J. Barnes called him "a man of sound principles and judgment, whose word in discussion always commanded respect."

At the Sunday meeting of the Worthing brotherhood, at the Literary Institute, members stood in silence to remember him and C. A. Kerry said "We are poorer by his passing, but the richer through his life."

Henry Jeffrey Thomas Brackley

Known as "Jeff", Henry Jeffrey Thomas Brackley (HJTB), according to the Worthing Voters' Lists, lived at 23, Chute Avenue, High Salvington, between 1965 and 1971. The son of a cabman, Henry Jeffrey Brackley and his wife, Annie (née Lindup), he was born on 18 August 1900 in Worthing. The family was living at 2, Thurlow Road, Worthing, at the time but by 1911 had moved to 10, Ann Street, Worthing. HJTB was a Worthing man all his life except for 8 years farming near Lewes,

In 1926 he married Violet Gladys Prince, a marriage that lasted 53 years. They had two daughters, Gill and Kay.

Alderman H. J. T. Brackley.
Worthing Herald 14 July 1967.

He was elected, unopposed, as an Independent candidate for Clifton Ward in January 1938.

HJTB was Mayor of the town in 1954-56 just as his uncle, Edward Anscombe Brackley, had been in 1938-40.

HJTB owned Salvington Hill Stores (The Village Shop, High Salvington) but, on reaching retirement, he sold the business in 1965 as "a slowing-down process". The shop was bought by J. R. King, of Horsham, and A. G. Granville, of Grand Avenue, Worthing, who intended to run it jointly and create more shopping space so as to "increase the range of supplies and provide greater variety at competitive prices."

HJTB said that disposing of the business would enable him to devote more time to his council and other local interests, which included Mayfield Youth Club, Worthing Yacht Club and the lifeboat. He was also a member of Tarring Priory Indoor Bowling Club where he played at county level.

He did not intend to give up his council work, saying, "The Council has been my life". At the time it was his 28th year on the Town Council. He added, "Although I may be getting old I am still young in mind."

On 7 October 1976, he was made an Honorary Alderman, an honour conferred on" those who have, in the opinion of the Council, rendered eminent services to the Council as past members of the Council, but who are not then members of the Council".

At the time of his death, he was the longest serving member of the Borough Council and been Father of the Council for 10 years.

HJTB died in the St. Barnabas Home on 6 December 1979. The funeral took place at Broadwater Parish Church.

He was described as "a loyal son of Worthing... conscientious and very knowledgeable".

Georgina Margaret Graham (1875-1962)

Known as 'Madge', Georgina Graham was the daughter of John Graham, artist, and the sister of Elizabeth, Lady Chalmers, artist, and of Katherine, wife of Frank Bramley (1857-1915), painter.

As might be expected, Madge, too, was an artist. Her obituary states that she exhibited her work in London from time to time.

Lady Chalmers (L) and 'Madge' Graham ®. Worthing Gazette 2 February 1949.

She worked in watercolours and also produced pen and ink humorous drawings. It was suggested that she had sketches published in 'Punch' but the magazine could find no reference to her when I enquired.

In middle age, influenced by the writings of H. G. Wells, she found inspiration in science fiction.

Madge lived with Dorothy Newman at 'Cerise', 1, Cherry Walk, High Salvington, between 1936 and the early 1940s while her sister, Elizabeth, was living with her daughter, Helen, at 'Cheyne Cottage', in West Hill, High Salvington. After Dorothy died in 1942 and Helen married, Madge went to live with Elizabeth at 'Cheyne Cottage', where she remained for the rest of her life.

Elizabeth Graham (Lady Chalmers) (1870-1951)

'A Hopeless Dawn' by Frank Bramley. www.tate.org.uk

Elizabeth Richardson Dickson Graham, Lady Chalmers, (LC) of 'Cheyne Cottage' West Hill, High Salvington, was born on 23 April 1870. She was the daughter of an artist, the sister of an artist, the sister-in-law of an artist and a respected artist in her own right.

Her father was John Graham of Huntingstile in Grasmere, her sister was Georgina Margaret Graham, known as 'Madge', and her brother-in-law was Frank Bramley (1857-1915) who was described as an English post-impressionist genre painter of the Newlyn School. He married Katherine Graham.

LC said of Bramley "He was a frail man and his output was not large, though unfailing in quality and sincerity." One of his best known paintings, 'A Hopeless Dawn', was considered by Leo Tolstoy to be "one of the world's greatest pictures".

At 'Cheyne Cottage', LC had a studio and a long picture gallery hung with her and her sister's work. At the end of the gallery hung a large painting by Bramley of LC and her baby entitled 'Helen Chalmers and her Mother'.

'Chrysanthemums' by Elizabeth, Lady Chalmers. www.invaluable.com

'Helen Chalmers and her Mother' by Frank Bramley (1857-1915). www.tate.org.uk

In the summer, when the cottage door was open, this picture could be seen by visitors walking along West Hill and there were frequent requests to be allowed to go in and look at it more closely. The painting now hangs in the Tate Gallery.

LC had married Charles Chalmers, later Sir Charles, a papermaker, on 18 October 1900 and Helen was born in 1907.

In 1931 LC was invited onto the Committee of Queen Mary's Institute of District Nursing.

Her art work was respected as a natural talent, remarkable for the easy suggestion of depth in its composition and its taste in colour. She painted in oils but also in a combination of charcoal and chalks and her subjects were chiefly portraits and flowers.

'Still Life of Roses' by Elizabeth, Lady Chalmers.
www.invaluable.com

She depicted her sister, Madge, in what was described as a "slightly tinted portrait drawing, alive in expression and rounded off nicely into the paper."

She often painted on glass and in 1949 Queen Mary accepted a small portrait of herself painted in this way by LC when it happened that the artist found herself in an adjoining box to the Queen at Drury Lane Theatre and was able to observe her.

LC's work was widely exhibited in galleries in London, the Midlands and in Scotland as well as in Worthing. In Scotland, she exhibited as a member of the Society of Women Artists at the National Gallery of Scotland in Edinburgh. In 1944, her portrait called 'Breton Peasant' was described in 'The Scotsman' as "a sensitive study". She even had one of her flower paintings on the cover of a seedsman's catalogue.

Although LC was of 'independent means', she was widowed in 1924 and does not always seem to have been really well off. She wrote a letter which appeared in the' Bath Chronicle and Weekly Gazette' on 29 December 1928 about the proposed abolition of quarter day payment of bills, saying, "it will be welcomed by those who depend on small salaries for they know what a constant worry and anxiety it is to put money on one side to meet the rent and rates and telephone and all the other bills that now run for three months or more." If regular bills could be paid once a month, she wrote, "people would know where they stood."

Lady Chalmers died on 1 December 1951 and was buried in Grange Cemetery, Edinburgh, with her husband and his family.

Sir William George Maxwell KBE CMG (1871-1959)

George Maxwell, as he preferred to be known, perhaps to avoid confusion with his father, was born on 9 June 1871 in Malacca in the Malay Peninsula, where his father, Sir William Edward Maxwell, was Lieutenant Governor.

Sir William George Maxwell KBE. CMG portrait by Lafayette. www.npg.org.uk

From the start, George was at the heart of British Colonial life. His grandfather, Sir Benson Maxwell, had been Chief Magistrate and George became the third generation in his family to enter the British Colonial Service in Malaya.

The history of Malaya is complicated but put very, very simply the Peninsula was made up of many Sultan-ruled States and because of its position on the major trading route between Gibraltar and Hong Kong Great Britain wanted a significant presence there, like the Portuguese and the Dutch before them.

From about 1824, by persuasion rather than by force, Britain increased her influence. The Sultans, having been assured that their status was not threatened, were willing to co-operate.

The policy of Her Majesty's Government was "not to interfere in the affairs of the Malay States unless where it becomes necessary for the suppression of piracy or the punishment of aggression on our people or territories."

The Peninsula consisted of the Straits Settlements, the Federated Malay States and the Unfederated Malay States.

The Settlements were transferred to the jurisdiction of the British Colonial Office in 1867 and became a Crown Colony, remaining so until 1946.

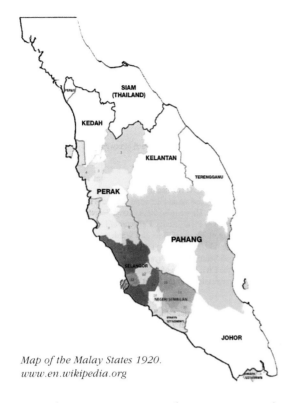

Map of the Malay States 1920.
www.en.wikipedia.org

The region thrived. Revenues nearly trebled, exports nearly doubled, the population increased (with the influx of immigrant workers) and roads, railways, hospitals, schools, postal services and savings banks were established. This was the world into which George Maxwell was born and in which he would spend his working life.

He was educated at Clifton College, Bristol, founded by Dr. John Percival in 1862. The aim of the school was to produce "children of varied but definite character" and develop young people who were "confident without arrogance and had a sense of responsibility for others."

The 1881 Census shows George living at 'The Hollies' in St Peter Port, Guernsey, with his American-born mother, Lillias (née Aberigh-MacKay), his maternal grandmother, Lucretia Aberigh-MacKay, and 5 younger brothers. The birthplaces of the children reveal how many times the family moved in the space of ten years. George was born in Malacca, Charleson in Scotland, Eric in India, Denis in Malaya, Gerald in Brighton and Peter in Guernsey.

George was the sort of boy that lived up to the principles of his school. In 1882, aged 11, he rescued a boy called Edwardes from drowning in Bordeaux Harbour. An account appeared in the Guernsey Star on 29 August and on 13 January 1883 the Portsmouth Evening News reported the presentation of a Royal Humane Society bronze medallion to George who was described as having behaved "so bravely and nobly".

George entered the British Colonial Service in 1891 as a junior officer in Perak.

On 23 August 1902, he married Florence Evelyn Stevenson, the daughter of Walter F. Stevenson, of Manila and Westhorpe in Kent at St. Mary's Church, Hendon. The church was decorated with white flowers and palms formed a canopy at the entrance. Rev. James Aberigh-Mackay, the bridegroom's maternal grandfather, officiated at the ceremony assisted by the Vicar, Rev. Newton Mant.

The six bridesmaids wore dresses of pale blue mousseline de soie trimmed with white lace. They also wore black chiffon hats and pearl and gold brooches, gifts of the bridegroom. The bride's dress was white crêpe de chine trimmed with Berthe Brussells appliqué, the gift of her mother. She carried a bouquet of white lilac and orange blossom.

*Lady Florence Maxwell.
Worthing Gazette 22 June 1938 p8.*

In 1906 George Maxwell was appointed Deputy Public Prosecutor in Singapore and two years later was promoted Solicitor General of the Straits Settlements and in the same year was called to the Bar and appointed Attorney General.

He was British adviser to the Kedah Government in 1909 and played an important role in the re-organisation of that State. Between 1914 and 1918 he was four times appointed Acting Colonial Secretary.

He was made a CMG (Companion of the Most Distinguished Order of St. Michael and St. George) in 1915.

In 1917 he was Acting Secretary to the High Commissioner for the Malay States and Brunei and in 1918 was Vice-Chairman for Food Control in the Sraits Settlements and the Federated Malay States (FMS) and General Adviser to the Johore Government.

In 1919 he returned to Perak as the British Resident. From 1920 until he retired in 1926 he was Chief Secretary to the Malay States.

His interest was natural history and he wrote a book called "In Malay Forests" as well as several legal works. He opened the Sultan Idris Teaching College in Tanjong, the first ever institution of higher education for the Malay people in the FMS. For his contribution to education, SMK Maxwell (School) in Kuala Lumpur was named after him as was Maxwell Hill in Taiping, Perak.

He was made a KBE (Knight Commander of the British Empire) on 3 June 1924.

The Maxwells moved to High Salvington in 1937 and lived at 'Chindles', Cherry Walk for over 20 years.

During WWII Sir George was in charge of the local Home Guard and Lady Maxwell organised the Durrington and Salvington 'Knitting for the Forces' group.

The Sultan Idris Training College in Tanjong. www.nisva.wordpress.com

Sir George died in Southlands Hospital, aged 88, on 22 August 1959 leaving two sons, Vernon Stevenson Maxwell and Clive Benson Maxwell and a grandson. Lady Maxwell pre-deceased him in 1957.

Reginald Arthur Mitchell (1891-1977)

Reginald Arthur Mitchell was a Worthing man all his life. He and his wife, Mildred Kate, née Crook, lived in Woodland Avenue, High Salvington, for about 26 years, firstly at no.3 and then, from around 1961 at no.11, 'Murrayfield'. They had three children, Eric, Joy and Betty.

Reginald Arthur Mitchell signing inaugural papers. Worthing Herald 22 May 1953.

Reginald Mitchell's father, Frederick William Mitchell, was a baker and confectioner, founding his business at 9, Montague Street, Worthing, in 1891, the year that Reginald was born on 12 November. Reginald's mother was Rhoda, née Castle.

Reginald Mitchell was a member of Worthing Council for 23 years, chairman of the bakery business, chairman of a cancer research trust and a member of the Rotary Club for 34 years until he broke his thigh in a fall in July 1976 and could no longer attend the meetings.

Music was very important to him and he belonged to Steyne Gardens Methodist Church Choir for 60 years.

He was elected Mayor of Worthing in Coronation year, 1953-54, immediately before H. J. T. Brackley, automatically becoming a Borough Magistrate for his term of office. He was made an Alderman in 1955. At the time of his death, he was president of the Worthing Mayors' Association.

He died on 7 January 1977 and the funeral took place at Steyne Gardens Methodist Church on Friday 14 January at 2.45.

Dr. Harold James Phillips (1897-1945)

Dr Harold James Phillips. Drawn by the author.

Dr. Phillips was born in Handsworth, Staffordshire on 17 December 1895. Because of his kind-heartedness and his cheerfulness, he was a well-liked man.

His father, George Tookey Phillips was a schoolmaster, teaching technical subjects. His mother was Eliza, née Belcher. In 1911, Harold, aged 15, was living with his parents and 17 year-old sister in Middleknock in Kilkenny, Ireland.

He qualified in Dublin, taking his MB, BSc (Public Health) and BCh in 1926, his MD in 1927 and his DPH in 1931.

In 1925, he married Mary Farrington at the Anglican church of St. Thomas in Werneth, Lancashire although Dr. Phillips' religion was Church of Ireland, as stated on the Irish 1911 census.

He was deputy Medical Officer of Health at Hastings between 1923 and 1935, assistant County Medical Officer in Kent from 1928 until 1931 and assistant Medical Officer of Health at Oldham.

Having held similar posts in Ashton-under-Lyme, he came to Worthing in May 1938 to succeed Dr. R. H. Wilshaw, who was retiring.

During the war, Dr. Phillips was a Surgeon Sub-Lieutenant in the Royal Navy Volunteer Reserve and saw service with the Cruiser Squadron of the First Sloop Flotilla.

Throughout the war, he spent two or three nights each week at the Civil Defence Control Room as head of the casualty service. He worked hard to maintain clinical services despite a shortage of staff and was deeply involved in the running of Swandean Isolation Hospital. His home was at 'Field House', Honeysuckle Lane, High Salvington, between

Dr. Phillips died in Southlands Hospital, at the early age of 48, after being ill for about seven or eight weeks.

CHAPTER TWO

A TUNNEL TRAGEDY

A woman's mutilated body, found in Cliftonville Tunnel, near Preston Park Station, on 9 February 1937, was identified as that of Isabella May Sims, wife of Arthur Mitford Sims, of 'Santa Barbara', Salvington Hill, High Salvington.

Forty-five year old Mrs. Sims had lived at 'Santa Barbara' for about a year and a half. Mr. Sims was a railway engineer who worked abroad. He had arrived back in England in October 1936 and was due to leave again in March 1937. It was arranged that Mrs. Sims would join him in October. Apparently, she had been abroad with him in the past.

She suffered from pains in her back and had been treated in Worthing and abroad. Arthur Sims said "The pains got more acute. Her health had deteriorated and she seemed dull at times". She had recently consulted a doctor.

On Tuesday, 9 February, the day of the tragedy, Mr. Sims had driven his wife into Worthing as she intended to do some shopping. He parked the car in Montague Street at about 11.30am. As agreed, he did not go with her to the shops, but went for a walk. Returning to the car at about 12.25, he noticed that she had put some fruit in the car. He waited until 2 o'clock but did not see his wife alive again.

An exhaustive inquiry was conducted by the Coroner, Charles Webb, with G. H. Snow, from the manager's office, representing the Southern Railway Company.

The body was found on the spur line at Preston Park. PC Maskell, of Brighton Police, said that the marks he found were consistent with a woman being run over by a train.

Cliftonville tunnel. www.gstatic.com

A typical 1930s train carriage door.
www.nz.pinterest.com

She was wearing a wedding ring engraved with the initials " I.M.J – A.M.S 7th August 1915".

The police surgeon, Dr. Sidney Hicks, said that death was due to compound fracture of the skull and laceration of the brain. Her right leg was almost severed.

Ralph Coomber, booking clerk at Worthing Central Station, remembered a lady dressed in grey (Mrs. Sims) taking a single ticket to Victoria. Just afterwards, another lady asked for two return tickets and the lady in grey asked if she could have a return ticket. He answered, "Certainly, madam. Are you coming back?" She replied, "No" and he said "Then there is no reason to take a return."

Frank Mappett, passenger guard on the 11.30am train from West Worthing to Victoria, said that there were few passengers on it and some compartments were empty. It was brightly lit and he demonstrated that the doors could not be opened from the inside but that one had to draw down the window, place a hand outside and turn the handle right round. There was no sign that any doors had been opened. All were in working order.

Mr Mappett had examined the train at Haywards Heath and again at Victoria and found no signs of a struggle. No-one had reported a disturbance to him. Mrs. Sims' handbag lay on the passenger seat with nothing missing from it. One report claimed it held 19s 7½d and the single ticket to Victoria while another stated that it contained £3 and a diary. No suicide note was found.

The Coroner, summing up, said that he had considered the possibility of foul play but thought that circumstances were against it. There was no sign of a struggle, or of theft, and the doors were secure. The possibility that the act was intentional was supported by the single ticket and that it had occurred in the first tunnel.

He said, "We do not always know the thoughts of other people, and it may be that Mrs. Sims was brooding over some worse development of those pains in her back." Consequently, he concluded that Isabella Sims had "committed suicide by throwing herself from a Worthing – London train".

The Coroner, Jury and G. H. Snow all expressed deep sympathy with Mr. Sims, who had been overcome with emotion during the inquest.

CHAPTER THREE

THE HOUSEKEEPER'S STORY

Mrs Elizabeth Ricketts, aged 72, lived at 'Southwold', a bungalow on Salvington Hill after which Southwold Close was named. A frail woman, she had been employed as caretaker-housekeeper for the owners, Dr Harold Albert Walker, a physician and surgeon, and his wife for the past three years. At the time of the following events, the Walkers were at their London home, 102, Fortress Road, NW5, and Mrs Ricketts was living alone at 'Southwold'.

During the early part of February 1931, neighbours were concerned that they had not seen the housekeeper for some days. On Saturday, 7 February, Charles Tudor Jones of 'Tylecote', Salvington Hill, went round to 'Southwold'. The door being open, he made his way to the back bedroom – and called for the police immediately.

Southwold Close. 'Southwold' was in the centre of the picture. Photograph by the author 2017.

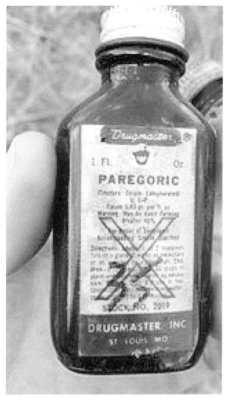

A bottle of paregoric. www.en.wikipedia.org

PC Bracken, of Durrington, found that the bed was unoccupied but the room was in "considerable disorder". Clothes were all over the floor together with a broken picture. There was a box of spent matches in the fender and a clay pipe and some shag tobacco on the mantelpiece. Mrs Ricketts, wearing only a few underclothes and a short woollen jacket, lay on her back on the floor with her head and shoulders under a dressing chest. There was blood on the floor, walls, and bed besides on the body.

Because it was possible that this was a murder investigation, an inquest was held at the Fire Station and presided over by the West Sussex Coroner, F. W. Butler. A police surgeon, Dr. W.O.Pitt, had examined the body in the bedroom and the next day had performed a post-mortem. He found a 3" long graze on Mrs Ricketts' left cheek, a 1" wound on her right eyebrow and a ½" wound on the back of her head. Her hair was singed on the right side of her forehead.

Witnesses were called to form a picture of the housekeeper's last days.

Her employer, Mrs Lucy Elizabeth Walker, said that she had not seen Mrs Ricketts since 30 September 1930 but that she wrote every week. Mrs Ricketts had written on 4 February to say that she was not well, feeling giddy and afraid of falling. A full bottle of paregoric had been found in the scullery and an empty bottle in a cupboard. This was a common medicine at the time used as a pain-killer. Its active ingredient was powdered opium. Mrs Walker told the Coroner that she knew her housekeeper took paregoric and that she smoked but had never known her to be drunk.

The jobbing gardener at 'Southwold', Bernard John Coote, told the Coroner that he had last worked there on 26 January and Mrs Ricketts had told him she had not slept for the past 3 or 4 nights and did not think she could go on living alone at the bungalow much longer. He described her as more depressed than usual.

On 1 February, Florence Mary Wheeler, of 'The Limes', was asked by Mrs Ricketts if she would change a library book for her and get her some medicine which she did. Taking the things to the bungalow, she got no reply so left them on the front door step. Later that day smoke was seen coming from the chimney of 'Southwold'.

Mrs Harriett Northcut Rutt, a nurse, of 'Purleigh' higher up Salvington Hill, said she had seen Mrs Ricketts walking with little control of her limbs as though drunk. Another witness said she noticed that the housekeeper walked with her hand on the wall for support.

Mrs Jessie Oldham, of 'Vega', next door to 'Southwold', saw Mrs Ricketts getting coal from the shed while in a half-clothed state and sent her maid, Marjorie Marion Needham, to see if she could help. The back door was open. The maid went in and called but there was no reply. She put the library book and medicine she had found on the front step on to the scullery table and left.

It was at Mrs Oldham's suggestion that Charles Tudor Jones had entered the bungalow and found the body.

The post-mortem revealed that Mrs Ricketts' body was emaciated and her heart was fatty but there was "no active disorder of organs". Dr Pitts estimated that because of the darkness of the blood she was feverish which caused confusion and that the wounds had been inflicted by her falling from an upright position, hitting her head on a corner of the bed. Dazed, she had crawled beneath the dressing chest. She had been dead about 48 hours when he first examined her.

The Coroner asked him if the wounds had been fatal. The doctor replied that in his opinion they were not. She had died of exposure and shock.

The verdict was Misadventure.

CHAPTER FOUR

TUDOR LODGE CHILDREN'S HOTEL

Standing on the north side of Palmers Way, off Salvington Hill, High Salvington, 'Tudor Lodge' was run mainly as a hotel for children of overseas parents, who would otherwise have had to remain at boarding school during the holidays or stay with reluctant relatives.

The hotel had a good reputation and a happy atmosphere and applicants often had to be turned away when there was a full house.

Situated 260ft above sea level, 'Tudor Lodge' had a view from the

Children playing in the grounds of 'Tudor Lodge'. Worthing Herald 22 April 1956.

balcony that encompassed 72 miles of coastline. It was run by jolly, 65 year-old Reginald Henry Ambrose, a retired accountant, and his wife, Dorothy, née Taylor, known to the children as Uncle Reg and Auntie Dorothy. In 1952 they had modernised the house and it could accommodate 20 children, of ages ranging between 2 and 10 years. The Ambrose's own child, Roland, a pilot, had been killed on active service in WWI at the age of 19.

Dorothy Ambrose was a trained children's dietician and she did all the cooking. The four nurses who looked after the children were often recent school-leavers whom Dorothy trained herself.

A typical day began early for Mr and Mrs Ambrose who rose at 5.15am. The children were all dressed and ready for breakfast by 8.30am and, afterwards, in good weather, they either played in the garden, which had swings, slides and a sandpit, with the nurses joining in the fun, or were taken out by Mr Ambrose in his large, beige estate car to the beach or the Downs. Indoors, there was a playroom that was the largest of its kind in the country plentifully supplied with 2 large rocking horses, toys, books and games of all kinds. Everything was provided. The children were not allowed to bring their own toys, perhaps for fear of introducing infection. The hotel boasted that there had been no epidemics here and parents were asked to provide a certificate of health for each child.

Lunch was at 12.45 and then there would be a nap followed by more play or outings (Arundel Castle was a favourite) until high tea or supper between 6pm and 7pm before the children were bathed.

Spoilt children were not pampered. All were treated with kindness but firmly and the atmosphere was encapsulated in the framed silhouette of a small girl dancing, called 'Joy', which hung in the hall of 'Tudor Lodge'.

In the Herald article it was mentioned that it was Reginald Ambrose's intention, within the next year, to extend the house to accommodate even more children. Whether this happened or not, the hotel closed and the house had changed hands by 1960.

The same article also reported that some of the young guests in April 1956 were those whose parents had been invited to attend the marriage of Prince Rainier, of Monaco, to film actress, Grace Kelly.

Children and nurses in the garden. Worthing Herald 22 April 1956.

Abdul and Adil Ayjan, of Iraq at 'Tudor Lodge'. Worthing Herald 22 April 1956.

CHAPTER FIVE

NUTSHELLS

1919

Southdown Motor Services Ltd., announced that on the first Saturday in June their service to High Salvington would be resumed after nearly three years.

Worthing Gazette 4 June 1919 p3

1919

A general cook was required, near London, for the middle of September, with good wages and conditions. Those interested needed to reply to 'Gorse Cottage', High Salvington. A Mrs Chapman was living at that address.

Worthing Gazette 20 August 1919 p8; Worthing Blue Book 1918/19

1919

A High Salvington 4-bedroomed accommodation was advertised with the special feature of indoor sanitation!

Worthing Gazette 26 November 1919 p8

1919

George Emmerson, of 'The Suntrap', Salvington Hill, (site of 'Eskdale'), a demobilised Royal Air Force officer, pleaded 'Not guilty' to driving a motor cycle and sidecar at a dangerous speed in Broadwater Road. He said that he thought he was going at 18 miles per hour but Constable Abbott disagreed, estimating his speed to be more than 30 miles per hour. The defendant was increasing his speed slightly, he said, to pass a car when the policeman stopped him. He said he was sorry and the Bench gave him the benefit of the doubt, only ordering him to pay costs.

Worthing Gazette 31 December 1919

1921

H. E. Warren-Williams, of 'The Oaks', Furze Road, was fined £2 for driving his motor vehicle along Goring Lane at the excessive speed of 29 miles an hour!

Worthing Gazette 14 September 1921

1923

At a dog show in Broadwater, organised by the Sussex Canine Association, 'Darkie Pip', belonging to Mrs A. Brangwyn, of 'Little Castle', Salvington Hill, took first prize in the category "Any variety not previously classified".

Worthing Gazette 27 June 1923

1923

James Victor Gorman was acquitted of stealing chickens from Southdown Poultry Farm, Wellingham Lane, but the owner, George Richard Hedges, further accused him of using "a false certificate of character" to gain employment at the farm. Gorman had told George Hedges that he had shown him a true copy of the original, which he had lost. Francis Kelly, his previous employer, stated that he had not given him a reference. Gorman was ordered to pay a £10 fine or go to prison for two months. He was given a week to pay.

Worthing Gazette 11 July 1923

1924

Southdown Motor Services Ltd. said that, although the service from Worthing to the Thomas a Beckett was well patronised, the portion to High Salvington was not, being mostly "pleasure traffic and uphill".

Worthing Gazette 26 March 1924

1924

It was reported that "unless otherwise permitted by the Minister of Health" the supply of water to the Borough from the works purchased by the Corporation from Alfred Charles Jackson in 1922 would cease after 20 July 1925. Because of the extra demand for water due to an increasing population, it was planned to lay pipes 9 inches in diameter "in the (Arundel) road (sic) to an elevated tank having its overflow at about 400 feet above Ordnance Datum into a re-inforced (sic) concrete covered reservoir to be constructed on the land at High Salvington purchased by the Corporation from Mr Jackson, with small tank thereon."

Worthing Gazette 4 June 1924

1924

The first annual meeting of the London and Home Counties Branch of the Libraries Association was held in Worthing. The delegates were given a tour of the area, going to Findon and on to High Salvington, where they were the guests of Mrs. Chapman at 'Mill View'.

Worthing Gazette 4 June 1924

1924

Eggs, fresh daily from Woodward's Commercial Egg Farm, High Salvington, were sold at Leal's Creameries, 43, Warwick Road, Worthing. Extolled for containing the health-giving A and B vitamins, they were also intended for sale to farmers and poultry breeders.

Worthing Gazette 25 June 1924

1924

Juveniles of Court Pride of Worthing, (junior members of the Ancient Order of Foresters) were taken by motor coach to the Downs for the afternoon. Almost 60 children and some parents had tea at the Bungalow Tea Rooms, High Salvington. After games and races, three cheers were given for the Secretary, Mrs Jeyes, and the committee.

Worthing Gazette 25 June 1924

1924

It was reported that to celebrate the 150th birthday of (High) Salvington Mill "the occasion is to be marked with a monster birthday cake with a candle for each of those 150 years of existence." Throughout the month the Mill would be open and "instruction talks" about its construction would be given.

Until a church was built at High Salvington, Evensong would be held in the "Round House".

Worthing Gazette 1924

1924

John Murray Roberts, of 'Mill View', Mill Lane, was involved in an accident at Broadwater. Trying to pass a Southdown bus, he drove his car onto the pavement and crashed into a fence on the west side of the railway bridge. The fence was broken down and the front of the car, including mudguards and radiator, suffered damage.

Worthing Gazette 13 August 1924

1924

Residents were complaining so much about the state of the roads in High Salvington that members of the Highways Committee went to see for themselves on 23 July. The result was a decision to widen the road at the top of the hill and make "certain other improvements" and the Surveyor was asked to estimate the cost. At their August meeting, the plans were approved and would be carried out at a cost of £165 3s.

Worthing Gazette 13 August 1924

1924

Every August, the Established and Free Churches of Worthing had, for many years, organised holiday gatherings for the children. Besides church services and prayers, they were taken up to the Downs every Saturday. On this occasion, they had a picnic, played games and had tea at High Salvington Windmill.

Worthing Gazette 13 August 1924

1924

Buses on the High Salvington route went past the Cupressus Poultry Farm, Durrington, run by Ernest Spruzen, and put passengers down at the entrance. If they made purchases amounting to £1 the single bus fare from Worthing would be repaid.

Worthing Gazette 31 December 1924

1925

'Restharrow', in Gorse Lane, "a commodious residence with outbuildings and terrace gardens" and 'The Retreat' , in the Mill grounds, were offered for sale but were both withdrawn when they did not reach their reserves of £2,700 and £875 respectively. They would be sold instead by private treaty.

Worthing Gazette 29 April 1925

1925

At the Windmill, a "charming furnished bungalow consisting of 3 bedrooms, a large sitting room and kitchen", was advertised for the month of July for 3½ guineas rent.

Worthing Gazette 1 July 1925

1925

Worthing Corporation invited tenders for the construction of two covered re-enforced concrete reservoirs at Durrington and high Salvington, each of 500,000 gallons capacity. The tenders were to be endorsed "Service Reservoirs" and delivered to the Municipal Offices on or before 10am on Monday 16th "proximo" (i.e "next month")

Worthing Gazette 14 October 1925

1925

High Salvington was not part of Worthing Borough until 1929 and it seems that before then there was no regular rubbish collection here. In November 1925, Robert Henry Gardner, of 'Pine Acre', Furze Road, wrote to the Council drawing its attention to an increasing plague of rats which were "a discomfort to residents and likely to prove a serious menace to health". The presence of rats, he said, was due largely to "the promiscuous manner in which house and garden refuse was thrown into the fields and hedges". It was his opinion that the only satisfactory method of dealing with the matter was the institution of a periodical house to house collection.

Worthing Gazette 4 November 1925 p7

1927

Windmill House Agency appeared in directories from the late 1920s until the early 1930s.

Worthing Gazette 15 June 1927

1930s

Derek Amey was the builder who constructed many of the bungalows in Mill Lane in the 1960s and himself lived at 'Dawn', Mill Lane.

West Sussex Record Office

The Windmill House Agency.
Worthing Gazette 15 June 1927.

1930s

Before WWII just 12 people across Sussex (East and West) had a television set. One of the first was in Worthing in 1936. There was also one in High Salvington.

Worthing Journal

1931

Patching & Co., offered 'Thyme Bank', in Mill Lane, High Salvington, for sale. Described as being "between the Chalk Pit and the Mill", the accommodation consisted of "Lounge, hall, large reception room, four bedrooms, bathroom, kitchen, scullery and usual offices. Central heating, garage, electric light and power, gas, main water. Frontage about 86 feet, also a BUILDING PLOT ADJOINING frontage about 114 feet WITH VACANT POSSESSION."

Presumably, the buyer was Harry Percival Firkins as directories show him living there in 1932.

Worthing Gazette 11 February 1931

1931

On 18 March, the freehold business known as 'The Rainbow Café', Salvington Hill, was offered for sale by Jordan & Cook. It was advertised as having "a frontage of about 48ft., and comprising teashop with two large show windows, partly screened off for service, large room at side divided into living-room and two bed cubicles, lavatory accommodation; electric light, gas, main water, central heating, together with garden in rear 24ft x 85ft." It is described in the advertisement as being "within a few yards of main Portsmouth Road."

In directories for 1929/30, the café was being run by Mrs Alice Lucy Heden. She was born in about 1883 and married Edward Arthur Heden, who was in the Indian Police. In 1921, Mr and Mrs Heden with their son, aged 1, and daughter, 5, arrived in London on board "The City of Marseilles" from Calcutta but Edward Heden died in India on 27 February 1923 and was buried in Calcutta.

Presumably, Alice ran the 'The Rainbow Café' to provide for her children. The sale does not seem to have gone through as she is still listed as being there in 1932/33. However, in the 1939 Register the café has "No residential occupation" and it is owned by Highfield and Sompting Dairies, which, although the café was on the other side of Salvington Hill, establishes a link with the present day Village Shop.

Directories for Worthing, 1939 Register (Findmypast.co.uk); UK Incoming Passenger Lists (Ancestry.co.uk)

1932

High Salvington branch of the League of Nations was well supported. At the Annual Meeting on 7 March 1932 at the Dairy Pavilion, High Salvington, Mr Kennelly, presiding, announced that 18 new members had joined in the last year which meant that almost every resident belonged. The hon. treasurer, Tudor

Jones, reported a balance in hand of £10 15s. Other members included F. Bailey, hon. secretary, Kate Coast, chairman, R. G. Martin, MA, chairman elect, Councillor F. R. Cripps, vice-chairman, Miss Stedman, hon. minutes and subscriptions secretary, Francis Mitchell, auditor, Mrs Tischbrock, BA and Miss Berry, hon. Collectors. Mrs Daniel, Miss Taylor and Miss Gostick were also members.

Worthing Gazette 9 March 1932 p11

1936

In January 1936, Worthing business and private properties were radically revalued upwards and this sparked a 'rate rebellion' culminating in a High Court case which the ratepayers lost. High Salvington, which had been part of the Borough since 1929, was affected.

Worthing Council was thought to be 'weak' and at the beck and call of West Sussex County Council instead of being on the side of the ratepayers, who were very angry in consequence.

Frank Redgrave Cripps, of 'The Droveway', Heather Lane, himself a Worthing councillor, was so shocked by the ratepayers resentment against the council that he wrote a letter to the Herald in an attempt to rectify the "amazing ignorance of local government on the part of the general public.

An incensed ratepayer had accused him of "doing well out of being on the (Rate) Assessment Committee" and when he asked her "How?" she replied, "Well, don't you get a fee for each case, as well as your salary as a member of the County Council?"

Another appellant against the rate increases was heard to tell other waiting protesters "They're all enjoying themselves in there at our expense" – a reference to the councillors who had been hearing the complaints having paused for refreshment.

Mr. Cripps wrote "The truth was that after a long and depressing day the Committee was having a cup of tea at the expense of Alderman Carmichael, whose generosity is proverbial."

In addition, he wanted to scotch the "widespread and obstinately held idea that councillors got some material advantage from their position" and went on "May I suggest, sir, that the heads of all schools should get some competent person to talk to the senior pupils about the working of councils and other statutory bodies, so that the next generation may not be deceived by catchwords."

In conclusion, he wrote, "Councillors get no salary, fares, allowances, free meals or lower rates."

Worthing Herald 25 July 1936

1938

The following information for this year is taken from a book called 'Worthing A Survey of Times Past and Present' edited by Councillor F. W. H. Migeod CC FRGS FRAI. It was compiled by local authors, each writing a chapter on a subject familiar to them, following the 43rd Congress of the South Eastern Union of Scientific Societies which was held in Worthing between 21 and 25 June 1938.

"Modern amenities are now available for houses built above the 300 foot mark, as at High Salvington..." Salvington Hill is quoted as "rising to 457 feet."

Chapter 'A Regional Survey of the Neighbourhood of Worthing by E. J. G. Bates BA p120

"Steps have ...been taken under the Scheme (Town Planning) to schedule further areas on Salvington Hill and Highdown for reservation as either public or private open spaces..."

At the time, Nancy Price and her supporters were campaigning for 59½ acres at the top of Honeysuckle Lane/ Salvington Hill to be saved from developers and become a public open space. The area is now The Sanctuary.

Chapter 'Open Spaces, Public Parks, Recreation Grounds and Trees in Streets' by Percy E. Harvey OBE AMICE Borough Engineer p141

"...a new concrete bridge has been completed on Field Place estate to carry a road from the Sea at Sea Place to cross Littlehampton Road, past the east end of Durrington, cross the Brighton-Arundel Road at Swandean Corner and end in High Salvington."

Chapter 'Town Planning' by Alderman Major-General R.E.Vaughan, CB Chairman of Town Planning and Housing Committee p163

The Municipal Isolation Hospital at Swandean is a much younger Institution (than Worthing Hospital) having its origins in 1897 when the house of that name at Salvington was acquired for the reception of patients suffering from infectious diseases..."

"The arrangements which obtained at Swandean in its early days would be thought to be primitive in the extreme. The acquisition of a wardmaid from the Worthing Hospital to act as a nurse was considered a very progressive thing and a matter for congratulation of those concerned. There was no specially trained fever nurse until 1905, when a properly qualified matron was appointed. An important event occurred in 1907 when the telephone was installed, enabling the matron to summon the Medical Superintendent in case of emergency.

Swandean. Sale catalogue 1 October 1895.

Before the advent of the telephone she had had to cycle down to Worthing for this purpose and, as the road led through wooded and secluded places, she generally carried a stout stick on the handle-bars of her bicycle. In the Hospital accounts of that period there is frequent mention of the hire of a cab for the conveyance of patients, which sounds very strange in these days when the word ambulance always implies a motor vehicle."

"The original Swandean was simply a large country house, and in its rooms no proper isolation of patients, or separation of those suffering from different complaints was possible. It became necessary to erect proper wards away from the house, and in the last twelve months further additions have been made, and the house itself has been practically reconstructed and extended at a total cost of £35,000. When completed in 1938, the main building will house the nursing and domestic staff, while in the grounds will be six ward pavilions, a laundry and disinfectant block, a mortuary, a small discharge building and a porter's lodge. One of the wards will be divided into cubicles in accordance with modern fever hospital practice."

Chapter 'The Health and Health Services of Worthing' by Cyril G. Eastwood BSc MB ChB MRCS LRCP DPH Assistant Medical Officer of Health pp172-173

"When the Parishes of Goring and Durrington (including High Salvington) were incorporated into the Borough in 1929 they were without any sewerage system.

Their combined area amounted to 4,857 acres, and whilst it was largely rural in character, development was being rapidly pursued along the coast and on the southern slopes of Salvington Hill, and it became necessary to promote a scheme for dealing with the drainage."

Chapter 'The Drainage of Worthing' by Percy E. Harvey OBE AMInstCE Borough Engineer p184

The High Salvington Reservoir, included with a reservoir built by the West Worthing Waterworks Co. in about 1894 and a larger reservoir constructed in 1927 was part of the Patching Pumping Station Scheme authorised by Parliament in 1922 to augment the supply of water from the Broadwater Pumping Station.

"High Salvington Reservoir has a capacity of 500,000 gallons and is built at an elevation of 430 ft above ordnance datum, it supplies the high level districts and delivers a bulk supply to the Parish of Findon. The cost of the Patching, Durrington and High Salvington Scheme was £56,000."

Chapter 'The Water Supply of Worthing' by O. Kean AMICE AMIMechE MIWE Borough Water Engineer p194

High Salvington underground reservoir. Photograph by the author 2017.

"The Worthing (Motor Services) Company bought up (earlier horse-drawn bus services) and substituted a motor bus service between East Worthing and Tarring with an extension on some journeys to Durrington and High Salvington...

Service 4 is the old service purchased from Mr. Jay, but all buses now go beyond the Thomas a Beckett, Tarring, to either Durrington or High Salvington...

Experiments have been made with some gearless buses on the level roads in Worthing, where the transmission is made by an hydraulic apparatus instead of a gearbox. For this first experiment they were tried on the High Salvington route, but were very slow and uneconomical on the long climb from Durrington to High Salvington, and now they are only employed on roads which are practically level from end to end."

Chapter 'Road Services' by A.D. Mackenzie pp212, 213 and 215

(Mr. Mackenzie was a consulting engineer in London, who was asked in 1907 to manage the ailing Worthing Motor Services Omnibus Company. He and another engineer, A.E.Cannon, put the company on a sound footing and in 1915 a new company was formed – Southdown Motor Services Ltd.)

"West Sussex Art Club. The members who form this club for the most part reside in Worthing and District. Meetings are held monthly, when a Professional Artist is invited to criticise the work of about fifty members. The general standard of the work is high and great progress in every department has been made during the last few years. It would be most difficult to find a more enthusiastic body of Artists. An annual exhibition is held in the town."

A. D. Mackenzie. Drawn by the author.

According to Kelly's 1938 Directory for Worthing, Mrs A. Lakeman, of 'Uplands', Salvington Hill, was the club's secretary.

Chapter 'Art in Worthing' by Donald Sinclair AMC ARCA Principal, County School of Arts and Crafts, Worthing. P247

Example of a Savonarola chair. Google image.

1938

An auction of furniture and effects by Patching & Co. was held at 'The Halt', Palmers Way, High Salvington, on 22 June at 2.30pm. Items included a 7ft Spanish mahogany wardrobe, an early Italian set of carving chairs with gilt embossed leather seats and backs, a carved oak Sicilian chest and 2 Savonarola type monks' chairs.

Worthing Gazette June 1938

1938

On 29 June Jordan & Cook auctioned furniture and effects at 'Larks Spur', Mill Lane, High Salvington, which included a "well-made OAK SIDEBOARD ... a pianoforte by Charles Cadby ... and an old wall clock by Wilks". William Wilks was working in the late 18th century.

Worthing Gazette June 1938

1939

Walking past a copse in Mill Lane, in June, a group of boys saw, on the east side, a man hanging from the branch of a tree. They ran for help and in a nearby field found John Mills, the owner of Salvington Vineries. They told him the man had been talking and moving but when he was taken down he was dead. Mr Mills recognised him as Stephen Ruff, aged 63, of 1, Beaconsfield Terrace, Ashacre Terrace, Durrington. At the inquest, George Stephen Ruff said his father had lived in Worthing all his life and had been in good health until a cataract operation two years ago. He did not seem depressed or afraid of becoming blind. Mr Mills, however, said he had always been a quiet man but he thought that lately he had seemed "very down". The Coroner, F, W, Butler, asked the dead man's nephew, who lived with him,"Was there anything about him that suggested that he was not normal in his mind?" The reply was, "No". Dr. W. O. Pitt, giving evidence, said he could not be sure of the man's state of mind – which the Coroner accepted.

Worthing Gazette 22 June 1939 p11

1941

Miss Elizabeth Mary Pope, of 'Bermuda', Wellingham Lane, a member of St. Ambulance Nursing Division, was given a St. John's guard of honour when she married William Cochran Cochran, of Glasgow, elder son of the late Captain J. B. Cochran and Mrs Cochran, at Patching. She was given away by her grandmother, Mrs Jessie Pope. Her brother, J.C. Pope, was best man.

Worthing Gazette 26 February 1941 p5

William Cochran and Elizabeth Pope. Worthing Gazette 26 February 1941 p5.

1943

Drimnagh Nursery School.
Worthing Gazette
6 January 1943.

Worthing Gazette 6 January 1943

1943

Nora Humphrey, of 'Seadown', Furze Road, wrote to the local newspaper about a problem she had with her daughter's ration book. On 5 October 1942, when the girl reached her 5th birthday, her mother was required to change her ration book and the little girl was looking forward to the two ounces of tea a week to which she would be entitled. However, when mother and daughter went down to the Food Office they were told that no new ration books would be issued until they came out for everyone – in six months time. A long time to wait, especially, as Mrs Humphrey wrote, her daughter may be "a small child" but where tea is concerned "she is a little old lady!"

Worthing Gazette 6 January 1943

1945

Actress, Mary Merrall, was shown in a scene from 'The Gambler', a play developed from a story by Dostoyevsky, performed at the Embassy Theatre in the sketch opposite from 'Punch'. Mary Merrall, whose real name was Elsie Dyall, was married to actor Franklin Dyall and they lived at 'Cerise', no.1 Cherry Walk, High Salvington, in the late 1940s. Other members of her family lived there in the 1950s.

'Punch' 28 November 1945

1949

Following the sale of Onslow Vineries, Worthing, for £17,500, Frederick Walter Burtenshaw, of Boundary Road, Worthing, claimed £37 10s for tomato boxes and £7 for labour supplied, from Gerritt Jan Sap, a Dutchman, of Newling Way, High Salvington. Judge F. K. Archer, in the County Court, gave judgement for the plaintiff with regard to the £37 10s, and costs, but not for the £7 as there was no evidence of a contract of labour.

Worthing Gazette 13 February 1949

1951

A freehold detached semi-bungalow "in good order" with lounge, kitchen, bathroom, separate WC, four bedrooms (two on the first floor), a ½ acre garden and a fine view cost £4,450.

Worthing Gazette 5 December 1951

1960

"During a two year posting with a cable company to Ascension Island, John Packer, 24, whose mother lived at High Knoll, High Salvington, explored the volcanic landscape and found in a fissure a hand-blown bottle containing a message bearing the name Johnson and the date August 1840."

Worthing Journal Issue 70 October 2016 p14

1862

"A red brick stamped with the date 1777 was presented to Worthing Museum and Art Gallery. It came from Burts' Barn, High Salvington, which was due to be demolished."

Worthing Journal Issue 67 July 2016 p87

1965

"A glider made an emergency landing in a field off Honeysuckle Lane. The pilot who had been on a flight from Basingstoke to Shoreham, had to stay in the aircraft until a herd of curious cattle that surrounded it had been moved away."

Worthing Journal Issue 63 March 2016 p30

1965

Tony Stracey, 23, of High Salvington, nephew of property owner John Brazier, progressed from the excitement of motor-racing to the thrill of flying light aircraft and had just flown solo for the first time, in a Bolkow Junior. He was also a member of Worthing's in-shore power lifeboat crew.

Worthing Gazette 28 April 1965 p13

Tony Stracey. Worthing Gazette 21 April 1965.

1965

Roy Cullum was director of Materials Data Ltd., and he headed a team of engineering design executives that left London Airport for a tour of the United States to study trends in design. Their findings would be included in the Feliden Report on Design. He and his wife lived in Foxley Lane for about 30 years.

Worthing Gazette 19 May 1965 p13

Roy Cullum. Worthing Gazette 22 December 1965.

1965

Anita Lonsborough, MBE, Olympic gold medallist, opened the new swimming pool at Swandean Hospital (now Meadowfield) on 30 June. Wearing an azure blue swimsuit decorated with a small Union Jack, she swam three lengths using a variety of strokes. She admitted afterwards that it was very, very cold. "I didn't even breathe for the first length and a half", she said, as she put on her blue robe.

The pool, 40ft long and 20ft wide, sloped from 2ft 6ins to 7ft deep and held 12,000 gallons. Surrounded by turf and edged with rose-coloured paving, it had a solar heating system, a filtering chlorination plant and changing rooms at one end. The cost was £1,150.

The new swimming pool. Worthing Gazette 23 June 1965.

Before her swim, the guest of honour had toured the 400-bed hospital with the Matron, Miss Hilda Lonsdale, MBE, and had had lunch.

The speech of welcome was given by Alderman R. A. Mitchell, a resident of High Salvington and a former Mayor of Worthing.

Worthing Gazette 23 June 1965; Worthing Gazette 7 July 1965 p8

Anita Lonsbrough and Matron Hilda Lonsdale. Worthing Gazette 7 July 1965.

1966

"A row over the name chosen for Worthing's new Roman Catholic Church under construction at High Salvington was referred to the Archbishop of Westminster. The title 'St Michael's' upset Francis O'Hanlon, who had lived next door in a property also called 'St Michael's' for 32 years."

Worthing Journal Issue 70 October 2016 p10

1971

"A row erupted over whether pink paving stones should be laid in 'rural' High Salvington."

Worthing Journal Issue 64 April 2016 p19

1971

Roy Cullum and his wife, Pamela, were long-time residents of High Salvington. They lived at 33, Foxley Lane, from the mid 1960s until the early 1990s. In 1971, finding their home in the path of the proposed six-lane M27 (running parallel to the A27), they gathered together about 100 angry and dismayed people living nearby to attend a meeting at Durrington Church Hall on 11 January 1972 to decide how to deal with the problem – whether to form their own organisation or work through existing organisations in Worthing.

Worthing Gazette 22 December 1971 front page

1972

Arthur John Brewer, 60, of 3 Oak Close, was included in the New Year's Honours List. He became an MBE. He joined the civil service when he was 17, in the West Country. Before moving with his family to Worthing, he was manager of the Holloway employment exchange for eight years. For the past two years he had been manager of Worthing's employment office and of area offices at Chichester, Bognor and Littlehampton.

Worthing Gazette 5 January 1972

Arthur Brewer MBE. Worthing Gazette 5 January 1972.

"Planners 'No' to scheme at Salvington"

"Plans to redevelop the site of Shelley Cottage, Shelley Nursery and Southwold, Salvington Hill, have been rejected by Worthing Town Council's planning committee on the grounds that the proposed scheme for 11 houses and five bungalows would be over-development of the area. In making the decision the committee had to consider a number of objections from local residents."

Worthing Herald 8 September 1972 front page

1973

Godfrey Biron, of 7, Foxley Lane was the fourteenth boy from Worthing Boys' High School to qualify unconditionally for admission to Oxbridge – a record for the school. He was accepted by Queen's College, to read engineering.

Godfrey's mother was an ardent member of High Salvington Women's Institute and she compiled a scrapbook of its history between 1966 and 1986 – the first twenty years of its existence.

Worthing Herald 2 February 1973

1975

In December, Miss Florence Mabel Hodges celebrated her 104th birthday. Small, slight and still able to walk upstairs, she had been a resident of 'The Priory', South Street, Tarring, for nearly nine years. She was born in Dublin, one of 10 children, and came to England to train as a nurse at Bristol Royal Infirmary. When

Florence Hodges. Worthing Gazette 3 December 1975.

she retired from nursing she came to High Salvington and in the 1939 Register she was listed at 'Hadleigh', a house in Cherry Walk, carrying out "unpaid domestic duties". It was a large household consisting of Mary Geoghegan, an incapacitated widow, Helen R. MacEwan, a hospital nurse, Mabel Curtis, a children's nurse, (who later became Mrs Storey), James Western Ross, a travelling chartered secretary, and his wife, Gertrude, and three other persons, probably children at the time and still living, so their record is closed.

Miss Hodges continued to live at 'Hadleigh' until at least 1946 with Mr and Mrs Ross, although the other residents had changed.

Worthing Gazette 3 December 1975 p48, 1939 Register (Findmypast), Worthing Voters' Lists

1985

"Jill Richardson, of Clifton Road, Worthing, received £50 reward from a man who lived in Mill Lane, High Salvington, after handing in a leather wallet containing around £5,000 that she found on a Worthing – Chichester train."

Worthing Journal Issue 67 July 2016

1987

"Marion Haddock, of Maple Close, High Salvington, died at the age of 81. She joined the Worthing Telephone Exchange in 1935 and went on to supervise around 200 'Hello Girls' operating the switchboard before retiring in 1964.

Worthing Journal Issue 72 December 2016

Marion Haddock (née Brice).
Worthing Journal
Issue 72 December 2016.

CHAPTER SIX

HIGH SALVINGTON IN 1939

Introduction

This chapter paints a picture of High Salvington at the start of World War Two based on the 1939 Register, which was made available on Findmypast.co.uk in November 2015. A brief description of the National 1939 Register, as it was more correctly known, may be helpful here.

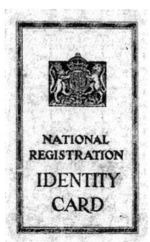

Ration Book cover and Identity Card. www.en.wikipedia.org

The war began on 3 September 1939 and the National Registration Act was given the royal assent on 5 September. Forms were sent to every British household and institution and it was the responsibility of the heads of households to enter the name, address, sex, age, marital status, employment and involvement, if any, in the armed and civilian services of every man, woman and child in their home.

National Registration Day was 29 September 1939 and a few days later 65,000 enumerators visited each household to collect the forms. After checking the entries with the head of the house, the enumerator took the forms away and copied the details into the official book whose pages we see on Findmypast.

The main reason for gathering the information was so that identity cards could be issued. The enumerators did this when they collected the forms. Later, ration books were issued and in the 1940s the register was used to identify those between certain ages who could be 'called-up' for service in the Army, Navy and Air Force. After the war, the new National Health Service used it extensively from 1948 for their records.

ADDRESS.	SCHEDULE.		SURNAMES AND OTHER NAMES.	O.V.S.P.I.	M. or F.	BIRTH.		S.M.W. or D.	PERSONAL OCCUPATION.	See INSTRUCTIONS
	No.	Sub. No.				Day.	Year.			
1	2	3		5	6	7	8	9	10	11

E.D. Letter Code EMKS   **Borough, U.D. or R.D.** Worthing   **Registration District and Sub-district**

This record is officially closed.

			Royall							
"Queen Mary" do	28	1	Bibby James	-	M	11 Oct	75	M	Engineer Director	
	28b	2	Bibby Constance O	-	F	31 Dec	92	M	Unpaid domestic duties	
		3	Gurney Joseph T	-	M	27 Dec	65	W	Methodist Minister (Retired)	
	✱	4	Gurney Hannah J	-	F	15 Nov	02	S	Not previously employed	
"Brindown" do	29	1	Richings Evelyn J M	-	F	9 Feb	72	D	Private means	
		2	Scott William J	-	M	21 Aug	68	S	Private means	
		3	Aston Mary C	-	F	23 May	90	M	Unpaid domestic duties	
3H "Lychgate Bratfield	30	1	Luke Alfred J	-	M	24 Dec	64	M	Chartered Civil Engineer (Retired)	
		2	Luke Mary	-	F	5 Dec	80	M	Unpaid domestic duties	
		3	Day Lily	-	F	SM 11		S	Domestic Servant	
3H "Lorthcaot" do	31	1	Butcher Elizabeth J	-	F	18 Mar	68	S	Elementary School Teacher	
		2	McCulloch Margaret	-	F	4 Feb	77	S	House property Manageress (Retired)	
3H "Speedwell" do	32	1	Daniels Florence H	-	F	19 Aug	67	W	Private means	
		2	Lawrence Jane E	-	F	5 Jan	60	W	Private means	
3H "Bay Mount" do	33	1	Prescott Percy P	-	M	7 Aug	74	M	Master Builder (Retired)	
		2	Prescott Agnes	-	F	23 Jan	78	M	Unpaid domestic duties	
WH "Hillcroft" Woodland Avenue	34	1	Cavell Frederic G	-	M	14 Feb	77	M	Builders Managing Director	
		2	Cavell Elizabeth F	-	F	29 Aug	75	M	Unpaid domestic duties	
		3	Cavell Elsie V	-	F	19 Aug	07	S	Unpaid domestic duties	
		4	Cavell Ronald F	-	M	14 Oct	14		Builders Assistant	
		5	FIELDER Sawtree Dorothy C	-	F	20 Sept	05	M	Unpaid domestic duties	

This record is officially closed.

This record is officially closed.

This record is officially closed.

| "Murrayfield" do | 36 | 1 | Halley Peter | - | M | 11 Dec | 89 | M | Shirting Manufacturing (Retired) | |
| | | 2 | Halley Kenneth | - | F | 8 Feb | 91 | M | Unpaid domestic duties | |

This record is officially closed.

This record is officially closed.

WA "Seaward" do	37	1	Newcomb Louisa M	-	F	23 Aug	77	W	Private means	
		2	SELIG Newcomb Edith M	-	F	12 May	10	S	Ladies hairdresser	
		3	Newcomb Emily G	-	F	17 May	02	S	Receptionist	
			Edward Charles	-	M	9 Feb	62	M	Draper etc (Retired)	
			Edward Lucie S	-	F					

This record is officially closed.

| WA "Merry oak" | | | Gouldsmith Arthur | - | M | | 72 | M | Bank Official (Retired) | A.R.P. Warden |
| | | | Gouldsmith Grace | - | F | 10 Feb | 75 | M | Unpaid domestic duties | |

This record is officially closed.

			Edwards Elizabeth	-	F	23 Apr	55	W	Private means	
4H8 "Highclere"	39		Comber Alec	-	M	19 May	01	M	Builders General Foreman	
	✱		Comber Olive L	-	F	13 Aug	01	M	Unpaid domestic duties	

This record is officially closed.

This record is officially closed.

This record is officially closed.

A page from the 1939 Register. www.findmypast.co.uk

Only the left hand page and one column of the right hand page can be seen because confidential patient information is written on the rest of the right hand page.

The Register is not a census but in some ways is similar. Censuses have been taken every ten years from 1801, as simple headcounts at first but gradually becoming more detailed documents. Because of the 100 Year Rule, a century must elapse from when it was compiled before a census can be made public in case people on it are still alive.

At the time of writing, the 1911 census is available but we will have to wait until January 2022 to see the 1921 census and another ten years after that to see the 1931 census. During the war, a 1941 census was not taken. Therefore, although the 1939 Register is not a census, it fills a considerable gap and, of course, is not bound by the 100 Year Rule. However, the records of those thought to be still living have been blacked out and bear the words 'This Record Is Officially Closed'.

The 1939 Register does not give people's places of birth or their relationship to the head of the household but does give exact dates of birth.

Some information is indecipherable because where splits in the paper occurred repairs were made with cellotape which has darkened with age. Names and addresses may be discovered by reading the transcription (though mistakes were made here) or by consulting a 1938/39 Kelly's Directory for Worthing but even so sometimes occupations cannot be made out.

The Register was kept updated until the 1990s. The most common change of information was when a woman married. Her maiden name was crossed out and her new surname was written above with, sometimes, the date of the marriage.

Other letters and numbers were added over time which even The National Archives in their online explanation of the Register admit to not understanding.

The column between the 'Surname' and the 'Male or Female' columns, however, can be interpreted. O V S P or I refer to the position of people in Institutions, of which High Salvington had two – Swandean Isolation Hospital and the South Coast Convalescent Home for Boys (Sun Hill Court, Mill Lane). 'O' meant an Officer, (such as the matron), 'V' was a Visitor, 'S' was a Servant, (for instance, a nurse,) 'P' was a (temporary) Patient and 'I' was an Inmate (a long-term patient).

ARP

ARP stood for Air Raid Precautions Warden. Those at High Salvington were:-

- Henry London, aged 40, of 'Como', in Salvington Hill.
- Geraldine Odling, 22, of 'Eskdale', Salvington Hill. She was the daughter of Dr. Francis Odling.
- Edgar Berry, 54, a retired cashier, of 'Ardrogué', Salvington Hill.
- Victor Ranston, 41, a commercial traveller, of 'Hill Brow Cottage' Salvington Hill.
- Doris Huggins, 39, wife of Dr Sydney Penrose Huggins, of 'Hugenden', Salvington Hill.
- Oliver Lovelock, 30, a chartered account, of 'Drimnagh', Hayling Rise.
- Karl Cotterill, 40, of 'Three Corners', West Way.
- Hallett J. W. Goodman, 67, a retired insurance officer, of 'Stoneways', Palmers Way.
- Dorothy Whitney, 49, a housekeeper at 'Binstead', Furze Road, the home of the Lloyd family.
- Walter Douglas-Jones, 54, owner of High Salvington Windmill, Furze Road.
- James Rogers, 64, a retired engineer, of 'Dawn', in Mill Lane.
- Arthur Gouldsmith, 58, a retired bank official, of 'Merry Oak', Woodland Avenue.
- William Jevons, 69, a schoolmaster, of 'Uplands Cottage', Uplands Avenue.
- Charles Snelling, 39, a mining engineer, of 'Hitherto', Foxley Lane.

PWC

Also appearing in the last column that can be seen on the Register are the letters PWC. This most likely stood for 'Post War Credits'. They were issued in April 1941 so the initials must have been added later. Post War Credits indicated that higher taxes were paid by members of the public in order to help the War Effort and would be repaid after the war.

Those in High Salvington who paid the higher taxes included Herbert Foster, a retired chartered accountant, who lived at 'Shuna', in Foxley Lane, Erica Dunkerley, the daughter of William Arthur Dunkerley, the author who wrote as John Oxenham, both at 'Conifers', in Heather Lane, Anne Simmonds, of 'Hill Top', in Mill Lane, Margaret Jones, of 'Tylecote', Salvington Hill, Stanley Mayers, Indian Police, retired, of 'Takiteezi', Salvington Hill and Alfred Lakeman, of 'Uplands' also in Salvington Hill.

The entire population of High Salvington should be shown in the 1939 Register because, by law, everyone was supposed to be included. A substantial fine could be imposed for refusing to be registered. High Salvington's population, therefore, can be fairly reliably put at about 1,060. However, with about 260 records closed that leaves around 800 open to view.

Oldest and youngest inhabitants

The oldest inhabitant was 88 year old Miss Elizabeth Emily Wright, born on 8 February 1851, the daughter of a coachman. She lived with 3 other elderly maiden ladies, all living on private means, and a servant at 'Parklea'. The youngest inhabitant was 2½ year old Ian Hunt, born in March 1937, who lived at 'Dawn' in Mill Lane.

The community consisted of some 260 dwellings set in 22 roads. One road was called Highlands Road in those days. This was the final part of Hayling Rise before it joined Salvington Hill and bears the same name.

There were a few vacant buildings, marked with a V on the far left of the page. 'Tudor Cottage' in Chute Way and 'The Drive' in Mill Lane were empty as was the house between 'Mesnard' and 'Hill Top'. On Salvington Hill, 'Café', (probably 'Rainbow Café') had "no residential occupation" but was owned by Highfield and Sompting Dairies

More than a quarter of those living in High Salvington in 1939 were described as being occupied with "Unpaid Domestic Duties" which, to my mind, is a derogatory term implying a servant who worked for nothing. In fact, they were the wives of the households and should be described as such, or as "Housewife" or even "Lady of the House". It is surprising, but there seems to have been little objection to the phrase. Those who preferred to be called "Housewife" included Alice Lidbetter, wife of a retired Local Government officer, living at 'West Ways', Hayling Rise, and Ethel High, wife of Leicester High, a master builder, of 'Sunnyside', Chute Way. Minnie Wade, of 'Metaville', Palmers Way, chose to be just "Wife".

About 130 people in High Salvington were retired, around 100 had private means and about 20 were incapacitated. Overall occupations ranged from domestic service (the largest category) and teaching and nursing (which together equalled domestic service) through secretarial work, farming, and the civil service to property. Those in unusual occupations I have a section to themselves at the end of this part of the book.

Not every resident is mentioned here – only those with more known about them than just age and residence.

This whole chapter is not scientific but, nevertheless, endeavours to present a fair and fascinating account of the inhabitants of High Salvington at a pivotal point in the country's history. The composition and way of life of the community would not be the same after the war.

Domestic Servants

Half the people in High Salvington employed in domestic service called themselves "Housekeepers" and some, like Lilian Lamb, at 'Southwold', Salvington Hill, where Sarah Tetley, a retired teacher lived, were both housekeeper and companion. Others in this category were Anne Taylor, at 'Normandy Lodge', Wellingham Lane, Edith Stroud's home, and Mary Savoury, in 86 year old, Emilie Sarter's home, 'Binswood' in Mill Lane.

'The Folly', in Mill Lane, the home of 71 year old William Carter, the retired director of Naval Construction at the Admiralty, was staffed on old-fashioned lines with Phyllis Spelding being responsible for domestic duties, and George Ryecroft, employed as both butler and chauffeur, while his wife, Hermine, was the lady's maid.

Constance Evans, later Mrs Lidbetter, was Sir George and Lady Maxwell's cook at 'Chindles', Cherry Walk, and Joan Altridge, later Mrs Saunders, was the cook at 'Rest Harrow', in Gorse Lane, where Michael and Dora Fenton lived.

Teachers

Over 20 teachers lived at High Salvington. Most of them were retired. Five lived in Salvington Hill. A married teaching couple Ernest and Kathleen Pledger lived at 'The Bend' in West Way.

Jeanie and Margaret Brown, probably sisters as their dates of birth were only two years apart, lived at 'Bescot', Foxley Lane. Mary Trapp, a domestic science teacher, lived at 'Southfield Cottage' in West Way.

Bertha Swaine, aged 40, the daughter of a 'watch motion maker', on her way to becoming a teacher began her own education at Londesborough School in Yorkshire in 1902 at the age of 5 years and 7 months and stayed until 26 October 1906 when her family left the village. I could not trace her further except for knowing that she lived at 'Sunrise' in Salvington Hill and became Mrs Wildman some time later.

Louise Read, Maude Thickbroom and Reginald Devereux all taught in London County Council Schools. They lived at 'Rowill', Palmers Way, 'Gai Logis' (interpreted as "Cheerful Home"), Newling Way and 'Fircroft', Salvington Hill, respectively.

Eveline Swanson, of 'Windover', Salvington Hill, was a friend of Kate Coast, headmistress of Worthing High School for Girls for 30 years, so possibly taught there also.

William Jevons was born in Duncton, Sussex, and in 1890 at the age of 21 was assistant master at a private preparatory (boarding) school in Great Malvern run by Hugh Edmund Wood. Frances Jevons, a domestic science teacher and possibly William's sister, lived with him at 'Uplands Cottage', Uplands Avenue.

Reginald Pratt, of Palmers Way, called his residence 'Myalla' after his childhood home in Australia. His father, Edward Pratt, of Cooma, New South Wales, was a 'pastoralist', that is, in other words, a sheep or cattle farmer. Reginald went to Hertford College, Oxford, gained his BA in 1902 and was assistant master at Dulwich College in 1906 and also taught at Carlisle Grammar School and Emmanuel School, Wandsworth. By 1911 Reginald was married with 2 children and teaching in Tiverton, Devon.

Ella Ransford, of 'Tanglewood', Gorse Lane, was born in Bath. She gained her MA at Cambridge, where she studied medieval and modern languages, and gained her BA at Dublin. Her subject was French and she was senior French mistress at Penarth County School for Girls and later at Belvedere School, Liverpool. She was particularly concerned that girls should have as good an education as boys and she was headmistress at Ipswich High School and Croydon High School for Girls. Both were GPDST schools. The

Ella Ransford's qualifications. Girls' Public Day School Trust.

initials stand for Girls' Public Day School Trust, which was founded in 1872 by influential women who recognised the lack of education opportunities for girls beyond elementary level. The aim of the Trust was to provide affordable day-school (non-boarding) for all classes of girls. Now called Girls' Day School Trust (GDST), the non-governmental organisation is still in existence today.

The Medical Profession

Doctors living in High Salvington included Laurance Philip Lassman, aged 26, living at 'Wyvern', Salvington Hill. A note in the Register states that he was "awaiting orders from the Emergency Commissioners". Regional Emergency/ Invasion Commissioners were representatives of the ARP, Police. Fire, Food, Voluntary Organisations, etc. Their role was to ensure that a good local defence scheme was in place and make sure the public was informed of arrangements in the event of invasion. Dr Lassman MB. BS London, 1938, MRCS Eng. was a Captain in the Royal Army Medical Corps during the war.

Dr Francis Crawford Odling MA., Camb. MRCS Eng., LRCP Lond., aged 45, had been a surgeon at Brighton and Hove Dispensary as well as Casualty Office and Resident Anaesthetist at St. Thomas' Hospital and in WWI had been a Temporary Surgeon Lieutenant in the Royal Navy. He lived at 'Eskdale', Salvington Hill. from the early 1930s, when it was called 'The Sun Trap', until the late 40s.

Also in Salvington Hill at 'Hugenden' was 66 year old, Dr Sydney Penrose Huggins, MRCS Eng.,1896, LRCP Lond., 1896, MB 1896 MD 1899 U. Lond., born in Middlesex. He appears in the UK Medical Register of 1923 in company with his father, Dr. Samuel Tillcot Huggins.

Dr. Olive Kendall Burnett, MD., MB., BS., MRCS.,LRCP, born in Aberdeenshire in 1896, had not been at 'Sunita', Hayling Rise very long as she was living in Battersea in 1934.

Dr Lucy Margaret Bell Nelson, MRCS Eng.1936, L 1936, M 1946 RCP Lond., MB BS 1936 U Lond. studied Obstetrics and Gynaecology. She qualified in England but chose to practice medicine in India. Perhaps she was visiting in 1939 at the time the Register was taken for the 1939 Medical Register gives her address as The Canada Hospital, Nasik, Bombay, India. At 'Four Winds', Hayling Rise she was with six people including Agnes Nelson, 59, who may have been Dr. Lucy's mother. In May 1946 the doctor went from London to Bombay on board the P&O ship 'Stratheden'. On the passenger list she gave her address as 'Hurstwood Cottage' Foxley Lane, High Salvington. According to the UK Medical Register for 1947 she was working at the Women's Christian Medical College, Ludhianna, Punjab, India, at a turbulent time in the country's history.

Dr Philip Cohen, aged 32, and his wife, Lily, neé Blumenfeld, lived with ten other Jewish people at 'Down House', Furze Road. His parents had both been born in Russia but he and his brothers and sisters were born in London. Philip qualified at St Bartholemew's Hospital.

Sun Hill Court Convalescent Home, Mill Lane. Worthing Library P005387.

Dr Julia Gottschalk, working at Sun Hill Court Convalescent Home for Boys was also Jewish. In the Register she describes herself as a "German Jewish refugee doctor acting as nurse". She studied and qualified at the University of Freiburg, which was founded in 1457, passing the "Staatsexamen", (translated as "State Examination"), which had to be taken by everyone trying to enter certain professions such as those of lawyer, teacher, doctor, pharmacist or nurse.

Percy Robert Cox-Martin, LDS. RCS., Eng. appears on the UK Dentist Registers 1879-1942 as having qualified in 1918. He lived at 'Greenroofs', Foxley Lane.

Many in High Salvington were involved in nursing but most were employed at Swandean Isolation Hospital and so cannot be counted as inhabitants of High Salvington because the staff, and patients, were a community within a community and lived elsewhere.

Nurses actually living in High Salvington were Helen R MacEwan, at 'Hadleigh', Cherry Walk, Janette Hastings, at 'Dunkeld', Furze Road, Jean Hutchinson, at the Mill with Mr and Mrs Douglas-Jones, Christine Payne, at 'Alee', Foxley Lane, and Catherine Hall at 'Greenheys', Salvington Hill.

'Jamaica Pioneer'. https://u.boat.net.

Children's nurses included Mabel J Curtis, living with a household of 10 people at 'Hadleigh', Cherry Walk (where Helen MacEwan, above, also lived), Rachel Doctor (used as a surname) in the Jewish household at 'Down House' and Mavis Q DaCosta, who arrived in the UK from Jamaica in May 1939 with Mrs Berthe Kelly and her children aged 8 and 6 and became part of the Kelly household at 'Oakden', Gorse Lane. The head of the family, Norman Augustine Kelly, was a telegraph engineer.

Three masseuses appear on the 1939 Register for High Salvington. Edith Jessie Goldsmith, who lived at 'Hillgarth', Salvington Hill, was born in Hastings in 1869. In the 1920s she was working in Tunbridge Wells and in 1934 she appears on the Register of Bio-Physical Assistants, the Society of Apothecaries of London, working at the Royal Sussex County Hospital at Brighton.

Ruth Jessie Good of 'Wairangi', Uplands Avenue, worked privately and was willing to visit her patients in their own homes and even take resident patients. Also, she indicated in the UK, Physiotherapy and Masseuse Register of 1934 that she was willing to treat National Health cases, which is interesting considering that the National Health Scheme was not launched until 1948.

Rose Maggie Farrington was born in 1870 and worked at Gloucester Royal Infirmary in the 1920s and in Worcester in the 1930s. She lived at 'The Field House', in Honeysuckle Lane with Harold Phillips, Worthing's Medical Officer of Health, and his wife.

Badge of a qualified masseuse. E-bay image.

All these physiotherapists were registered as members of CSMMG (Chartered Society of Masseuses and Medical Gymnasts) and CSP (Chartered Society of Physiotherapy). Each would have been given a badge, similar to the one illustrated, individually numbered on the reverse, when they qualified. Designs varied and this type of badge was issued between the 1920s and 1940s. The Latin motto 'Digna Sequi' means 'Follow Worthy Things'.

Engineers

Alfred Charles Jackson, a Quaker, was a retired mechanical engineer who was an influential man in the neighbourhood. He was born in Islington in 1868. His father was a tea merchant and his mother a school teacher. In 1906 he bought High Salvington Mill and the surrounding land which he sold in 1912 as forty-two building plots and so began the development of residential High Salvington. His engineering skills were such that he was commissioned to make prismatic compasses for the Government in WWI. In about 1931 he was on Worthing Town Council and was made an Alderman in 1936. His

Alfred Charles Jackson.
Drawn by the author.

hobby was making fine models of ships, some of which were exhibited at the Science Museum, South Kensington. He lived at 'Upper Dell', Heather Lane.

Joseph Traxler, of 'Court Green', in Mill Lane also described himself as a retired mechanical engineer, but in the 1911 England Census he was the manager of a public company dealing in house property and in the 1901 census he was a cycle engineer.

Rear Admiral James Mountfield, of 'The Downs', Salvington Hill, joined the Royal Navy in 1891 at the age of 20 in the new engine-room branch. His first ship was HMS Alexandra which had both sails and steam engines.

Ernest Mortlock Barton, of 'Lyndale', Broadview Gardens, was a retired civil engineer who, it was announced in the London Gazette of 2 October 1894, had been a successful candidate in an "Open Competitive Examination for the

HMS 'Alexandra'. National Maritime Museum.
Rear Admiral James Mountfield.
Worthing Gazette 6 July 1955.

situation of Draughtsman in the Department of the Director of engineers and Architectural Works in the Admiralty". He was awarded an OBE in 1920 for his services in the First War and in April 1921 he was elected a Member of the Institution of Civil Engineers. At the time he was Superintending Civil Engineer (Higher Grade) at H.M.Dockyard, Portsmouth.

In December 1921, Alfred James Luke,OBE, too, was elected a member of the Institution of Civil Engineers. His position was Superintending Civil Engineer and his place of work was H.M.Dockyard, Haulbawling, Ireland. When the Register was compiled he was living at 'Lychgate', Bost Hill.

Secretarial

Leila C Tournoff, the name of whose home is obscured by discoloured cellotape on the Register but was on the same page as those in Salvington Hill, was a shorthand typist, like Feo Violet Florentin Sachs, who lived at 'St. Bride's Dell' in Furze Road, but was born in Australia in 1896.

Secretaries included Ailsa Gibb, of 'Green Gates', Palmers Way who married Hilary Redgrave Cripps, son of Francis Redgrave Cripps, of 'The Droveway', Heather Lane, Gertrude Louisa Aldock, of 'Hill Top', in Mill Lane and Irene lily Margesson, at 'Reston', Furze Road, who was the daughter of retired Lt. Col. William George Margesson of Findon Place.

Findon Place. www.geograph.org.uk

School secretary, May Scott lived at Tanglewood' in Gorse Lane and Eliza Spencer, of 'Cintra', Heather Lane. was the secretary of Rev. Walter Spencer, chairman of the Southern Counties Convalescent Homes (of which Sun Hill Court was one).

At 'The Shanty', in the Mill grounds lived Melina Bokenham, who described herself as a stenographer.

Both the chartered secretaries in the Register were men. James W Ross lived at 'Hadleigh', Cherry Walk and William Henry Harries at Gorse Cottage, Gorse Lane. The latter was a Freemason, member of the New Concord Lodge (No. 813), London, from 1910.

Directors

Henry London, Maurice Goldwater and Maurice Rosner were all directors of clothing manufacturing companies. The latter had a government contract which probably meant that he made uniforms, etc. The first man lived at 'Como' in Salvington Hill while the other two lived at 'Down House', in Furze Road.

Joseph Arthur Mason, of 'Throstle Nest', Newling Way, was the director of his own cycle firm. He was a prominent man in Worthing being Mayor twice, in 1940-41 and 1945-46. See his biography in 'A History of High Salvington' Book 2, page 18.

Joseph Arthur Mason.
West Sussex Record Office MP 46.

Karl Cotterill was director of a firm of insurance brokers and lived at 'Three Corners', West Way.

Directorships usually come with age and may follow quite different starts in life. This was the case with Clarence Ford Elms. He was born on 12 January 1888 and baptized at St Mary's Church, Marylebone, on 4 March. His father, Robert, was a hair dresser. At the age of 17, Clarence was apprenticed on 8 June 1905 in the Merchant Navy to James P. Corry & Co. The term of the apprenticeship was to be 3 years. By August 1905 Clarence was in Australian waters aboard the 'Star of Scotland' sailing between Melbourne and Sydney and on the same ship in September 1906 between Wellington and Sydney. However, it seems that the life did not suit him because on 18 December 1906 his apprenticeship was cancelled. By 1920 Clarence was married with a 6 year old son. He, his wife, Margaret, and son, Jack, sailed from Avonmouth to Jamaica in January and his occupation on the passenger list

Clarence Ford Elms, crew member. www.ancestry.co.uk

was given as 'nil'. When they returned to Avonmouth in June 1920 he described his occupation as 'engineer'. In the 1939 Register he is the managing director of a Motor Garage Works and lived at 'Two Ways', Heather Lane.

William Victor Royle Baldwin, of 'Mont Dore', West Hill, was a numismatist (a dealer in coins and medals) and had had business premises in Twickenham and two sons who followed the same career. William was director of the business.

Herbert Archer. www.findmypast.co.uk

Herbert Archer, of 'Mill View', Heather Lane, was a newspaper man. He was the managing editor and a director of the newspaper company of T. R. Beckett, who published the Eastbourne Gazette and Herald and the Worthing Gazette and Herald.

Clerks

Cecil Charles Henry Grosse, a quality clerk with the petroleum board, had been born in Clapham, London. At the age of 11, he was a boarder at Lewisham House, Landerman Circus, Weston-Super-Mare, Somerset, with his 13 year old brother, Leonard, under the headmastership of Frederick George Confort. In WWI Cecil trained as a pilot at Greenwich in the RNAS (Royal Naval Air Services), flying an S.E 5 and achieved the rank of 2nd Lieutenant. He spent time in Africa between the wars but returned to the UK in 1930 and re-joined the RAF as ground support. He lived at 'Alberni', in West Hill.

Herbert Wood Barter, born in Leighton Buzzard, Bedfordshire, was a solicitors' clerk in the 1901 England Census and in the 1911 Census was Assistant Clerk to Finchley District Council. He was reported in the Hendon and Finchley Times of 26 June 1931 as having been appointed by a unanimous vote to Clerk of Finchley District Council. The newspaper described him as "of quiet demeanour" "but "undoubtedly a leader". The article concludes – "With the incorporation as a borough looming in the distance who shall say that Mr Wood Barter will not soon reach his ambition as a Town Clerk in the Borough of Finchley." He did achieve his ambition but had to retire due to ill health. He lived at 'Cobblestones', in Furze Road.

Children

Only a dozen children of school age are shown living in High Salvington in 1939. The oldest were two sixteen-year-olds, Aidan Cyril F O'Hanlon, of St Michael's, Hayling Rise, and Dorothy Howard at 'Morehall', Mill Lane.

David Price, 15, lived at 'Altwood', Hayling Rise, with his parents but other children were living in households where the surnames were different from their own. For instance, Joan Cameron, 15, and Doreen Maddison, 14, lived at 'The Cottage', in Heather Lane, the home of Miss Margot Douglas, and her housekeeper, Miss Elizabeth Farmer. This might mean that the two girls were evacuees.

Only one child is specifically registered as an evacuee and he was David William Knox, aged 6, who was billeted with Sir George and Lady Maxwell at 'Chindles', Cherry Walk.

Elsie Saunders, 15, lived with her parents, George and Ethel, at 'Elmcroft', Salvington Hill and another girl, Grace Carpenter, 11, who may or may not have been a relation.

Ronald Keys, 12, was living with widower, James Chennell, Miss Catherine Chennell, and widow, Mrs Edith King, who shared housekeeping duties with Miss Constance Barnard, at 'Birdseye View', Salvington Hill.

Elizabeth Phoebe Stern, 12, was registered with the Parsons family at 'Polrode', Salvington Hill. The head of the household, Reginald Parsons, is shown with his wife, Ada, and Cedric Simpson Parsons, aged 11. Mrs Ada Pretoria Parsons was the widow of George Herbert Bloye (see page 7 for his biography) with whom she also lived at 'Polrode'.

Grace Dunnachie, 12, lived with her bus driver father, at 'Midgham', in Uplands Avenue, and the youngest school age child in High Salvington was

Michael Brian S Gibson, aged 5, who lived with his parents, Edward and Kathleen, at 'Sea Vista', Mill Lane.

Farmers

Frank Ormond Soden DFC.
www.en.wikipedia.org

A map of c1785 shows that the area now called High Salvington was Durrington Farm, half of which was divided into strips of agricultural land and half, covered in furze (gorse bushes), which was used for grazing. In 1939 the farmers were retired and had farmed elsewhere.

In Gorse Lane was a retired dairy farmer, Isabel Florence Ransford, at 'Tanglewood', and a retired sheep farmer, Michael C N Fenton, at 'Rest Harrow'.

Percy Payne described himself as having dealt in "Farming and Land – specialising in poultry". He lived at 'Vega', Salvington Hill.

At 12, Broadview Gardens, was Frank Soden, farmer, born in London in 1863. His children were born in New Brunswick, Canada. One of his sons,

Frank Osmond Soden, was a pilot. Aged 21, he gained his Royal Aero Club Aviators' Certificate on 9 September 1916 flying a Grahame-White biplane at the Grahame-White School, Hendon. Later, he was awarded the DFC (Distinquished Flying Cross) and bar. He died in Kenya in 1961 and his obituary in the Ottawa Journal described him as a "Canadian-born British air ace".

A Spanish farmer and refugee, Antonio Pertinez, is registered at 'Hillcrest', in Gorse Lane, the home of Lt. Col. Henry Pritchard and his wife, Anna. Antonio's wife was also here. He and Clover Nancy Darvill de Nagy, from Hungary, married in Worthing in 1936. Clover had applied for British naturalisation. The papers are stored at the West Sussex Record Office but cannot be viewed until 2036.

Banking

George Ede M Lewin was a bank accountant living at 'Roughdown', Salvington Hill.

Frank Barber and Charles R Ingersol were bank officials and both lived in West Way – the former at 'Balgownie' and the latter at 'Conway'. Another bank official lived in Mill Lane at 'Cairn Cottage'. He was John H C Howie.

Three bank managers are on the 1939 Register, including George A Needham, born in 1874, had his home at 'Meadowfoot Cottage', Foxley Lane. Francis John Cumming of 'Cathmor', Palmers Way, was a witness in an Old Bailey trial in June 1911 when Charles Edward Hogg and Thomas Henry Butt were accused of deception and fraud. At the time Francis Cumming was chief cashier at Credit Lyonnaise, 4 Cockspur Street.

Lewis Morgan Jarman, son of an auctioneer and farmer, was born in Wales. He was a Freemason, being a member of the Lorne Lodge, Sutton, from 11 October 1919. His home was at 'Appledore', Cherry Walk.

Clothing

There are four drapers in the Register. Lilian Woodland was a fancy draper living at 'Sunnydene', West Way. A fancy draper would have sold straw hats, gloves and underclothes etc. whereas a draper was a seller of textile fabrics.

Richard Ernest Baxter Whitehall, draper, was born in Birmingham and had been a drapery buyer in Streatham, according to the 1911 England census. He lived at 'Arosa', West Hill.

Retired drapers, Mary K Nevin, born in Dublin, and Sarah A Wright both lived at 'Cissbury Cottage', West Hill.

At 'Como', Salvington Hill, was Samuel Freed, a wholesale milliner (hats) and at 'Swandean Corner', Salvington Hill, was Barbara Manning, dress designer, maker and seller.

John M White, a cotton manufacturer, lived at 'Larksfield' Furze Road, and Peter Hally, a shirting manufacturer, lived at 'Murrayfield', Foxley Lane.

Leon Robert, of 'Sunridge', Mill Lane, was a furrier, although earlier in his life he had been a farmer. His name at birth had been Leon Ou Reuven Doubnikoff. He was born on 31 January 1878 in Russia to parents Movsha and Bonnia (neé Rassia) Doubnikoff. He changed his name and referred to himself as English on a 1904 passenger list. He died in Sussex, aged 92.

Building

Four master builders resided at High Salvington in 1939. John Stuart Galbraith, lived at 'Windrush', Woodland Avenue, Leicester J High, at 'Sunnyside', Chute Way, Herbert C S Waller, at 'Finnistere', Palmers Way, and Percy Pescott, at 'Baymount', Bost Hill.

HIGH LEICESTER J. (repairs in all branches), Sunnyside, Chute way, High S. **TELEPHONE, SWANDEAN 709**

Leicester J High advertisement.
Kelly's Directory 1938.

John Galbraith, born in Stockton-on-Tees, Durham, went to New Zealand on 1 February 1893 on board the 'Ruahine', with his wife and two children – a 90 day voyage. Two more children were born in New Zealand before the family returned to the UK.

Percy Puttick Pescott, the son of a baker, was born in Stanley Road, Broadwater. He joined the RFC (Royal Flying Corps) on 13 June 1916 as a Fitter. He was promoted to Corporal on 1 April 1917. In 1918 he was transferred to the newly formed Royal Air Force and promoted again. According to the RAF Muster Roll, his pay was 5s a day (25p in today's money). He signed up for the 'Duration of the War' and was transferred to the RAF Reserve before discharge on 30 April 1920. The 1939 Register shows him still on the reserve list. He lived at 'Baymount', Bost Hill.

Others connected with buildings included a building estate sales rep., a general building , house property manager, and two estate agents.

Arthur Creighton Gibb, one time manager of the building dept. of Stepney Borough Council, lived at 'Green Gates', Palmers Way. His daughter, Ailsa, married Hilary Redgrave Cripps, the engineer son of Frank Redgrave Cripps, of 'The Droveway', Heather Lane.

Also living at 'Green Gates', was retired architect, Albert Samuel Manning. He had been born in the horse-racing town of Newmarket, in Suffolk, and was a Jockey Club Clerk. His father, James, had been Clerk of the Scales and agent to the Jockey Club.

Guest House Proprietors

High Salvington was an attractive place for visitors coming to the Downs and to the Windmill and there were several guest houses to accommodate them. All were run by women.

Caroline Darker, born in Dublin, the daughter of an Irish Army Captain, and Clara Home, together at 'Reston', in Furze Road, took paying guests.

The other places offering accommodation were family-run. Constance Marie Gostick and her sister, Alice, took guests at separate properties – 'Hill Top', Mill Lane, and 'Merrydown', Furze Close, respectively.

Olivia Clarke, jointly with her sister, Amelia, took visitors at 'Peverell', Furze Road. Emma and Lilian Moss, similarly accommodated guests at 'Wyvern', in Salvington Hill, and Eveline Maud Slingsby and her two sisters, Alice Gwendoline and Grace Winifred, ran a guest house and tea gardens at 'The Chalet', in Furze Road.

Civil Service

The civil service covers a wide range of employment from clerks to colonial governors which High Salvington residents mirrored.

Bessie Kate Brangwin of 'Overdale', Salvington Hill, was a clerk. Sisters, Theodora and Ruth How, were GPO clerks and lived with their mother, Winifred, at 'Downfold', in West Way.

Charles Sinkings, a 2nd division clerk, was born in Chertsey, where his father, James, was a master at Sir William Perkins' School. Charles lived at 'Upper Cote', in Furze Road.

'The Chalet', Furze Road.
Photo courtesy of Mary Steel 1989.

'Peverell', Furze Road. Worthing Library P005382.

Also in Furze Road, was Mary C. Bebb, a superintendent of typists, at 'Peverell'.

In Mill Lane resided Thomas Wreghitt Rank, at 'Kop View', and Harry Firkins at 'Thyme Bank'. Further up Mill Lane, Clara Home was in the habit of opening 'Reston' to the public for a couple of weeks each Christmas and New Year. She would set out tables with miniature figures arranged in the form of a pageant. In 1939-40, for instance, there were three tableaux, 'The Nativity', 'The Nation's Response to the King's Call to Prayer' and 'The Light Beyond the Sacrifice'. The money donated by visitors went to the British Red Cross. Harry Firkin's 12 year-old son, Roger, a chorister at Westminster Abbey, sang 'O Valiant Hearts' during the event.

Francis Augustine O'Hanlon, of St. Michael's, Hayling Rise, besides being a civil servant, was the driver of an ambulance and knew first aid. He also enjoyed writing and founded the 'West Sussex Writers' group which celebrated its 80th anniversary in Worthing in 2017 with a day-long seminar at Bohunt School, Broadwater, and a cake in the shape of an old style typewriter.

Sir William George Maxwell, KBE, who lived at 'Chindles', Cherry Walk, for about 29 years, was a colonial civil servant. (See page 14 for an account of his life).

Religious Callings

Men and women of various religious persuasions appeared on the 1939 Register. They include Alfred Thomas Greenwood, a retired Baptist minister, born in Yorkshire, who lived at 'Tudor Lodge', Palmers Way, Thomas Lloyd Page, a Methodist minister, living at 'Halkin', Woodland Avenue, Geraint Ashworth, Clerk in Holy Orders, at 'The Little House', Furze Road, and Winifred Agnes Galbraith, a missionary, at 'Joylands', Heather Lane.

Also missionaries were husband and wife, Thomas and Margaret (née Reid) Collins living at 'Kingfisher', Mill Lane, particularly concerned with work in Western Africa.

Ruth and James Alexander Stewart. Google images.

James Alexander Stewart and his wife (Doris) Ruth Mahan, whom he married in 1938 in Hungary, were Protestant missionaries. At the time of the 1939 Register they were living at 'Larkfield' in Furze Road. James, born in Glasgow in 1910, was fervent in his religious zeal. He began preaching publically at the age of 14 and was soon working for the London Open-Air Mission. He founded the Border Movement in 1928 and in the same year made his first visit to the United States and organised the European Evangelistic Crusade. The Stewarts moved to America in 1940 and, after the war, James was the first preacher from the Free World to go behind the Iron Curtain. In 1957 he founded Gospel Projects Inc. and took over the Russian Bible Society. He wrote over fifty books and pamphlets.

Abroad

Sidney Andrew Ford, born in Camberwell, was Political Assistant in the Anglo-Iranian Oil Company and retired to 'The Cottage' in West Way.

Stanley Roy Mayers, of West Dulwich, was in the Indian Police. Together with his new wife, Dorothy, and widowed mother-in-law, Helen Dennis, he travelled to Calcutta from London on board the 'Neuralia' in December 1919. At the time of the 1939 Register they were all three living at 'Takiteezi', in Salvington Hill.

Charles A Williams, who was born in Persia, was a retired Chinese Customs official and living at 'Broomfield', Salvington Hill.

The Delhi Durbar, 1911. www.en.wikipedia.org

The Delhi Durbar medal, 1911. www.Ancestry.co.uk

The son of a Scottish military officer and a mother born in India, Charles Fred Hilton Thomson joined the Hampshire Regiment in WWI and reached the rank of Major. His home was at 'The Halt', Palmers Way.

Rear Admiral James Mountfield was a naval engineer. He lived at 'The Downs', Salvington Hill. He joined the Royal Navy in 1891. He was eager to embrace the new steam power and his first ship HMS Alexandra had both masts and steam. From 1947 he was chairman of the local branch of the British Sailors' Society.

Henry Edward Pritchard of 'Hill Crest', Gorse Lane, was born in India and was baptised at a church in Secunderabad, Madras. His father was Henry Follett Pritchard, a Lieutenant in the Royal Horse Artillery at the time. Henry Edward Pritchard joined the Royal Irish Regiment in 1884 at the age of 22. In 1887 he was seconded for service with the Indian Staff Corps and promoted to Captain in 1896. He was a Major in the Indian Army in 1903 and Lt. Col., Commandant of the 82nd Punjabis, in 1910. He received the Delhi Durbar medal for his participation in the 1911 event that celebrated the coronation of King George V. In WWI he commanded the 10th Service Battalion of the Gloucestershire Regiment, training at Cheltenham and Salisbury Plain before arriving in France and fighting at the Battle of Loos in which most of his regiment perished. An account appears in the book 'In the Shadow of Lone Tree' by Nick Christian. Lt. Col. Pritchard left the Army in April 1919.

Solicitors

Harry S Inwood of 'Woburn Cottage', Salvington Hill', worked in Worthing. His father, at the same address, was an auctioneer.

Living at 'Pine Acre', Furze Road, in 1939, Robert Henry Gardner, gave his address as The Treasury, Whitehall, when he became a member of no. 779 Ferrers and Ivanhoe Freemasons Lodge, Ashby-de-la-Zouch, on 29 November 1898.

Sam Cook, a travelling solicitor, was also a Freemason. He was a member of no. 2696 Arcadian Lodge from 22 January 1907 when he was living at 95, Edgware Road, London. His home at High Salvington was 'South Cottage', Furze Road.

Charles Goldwater, LLB., Lond, was born in Gateshead, Durham and lived at 'Down House', in Furze Road. In 1943 he married a Miss Rosen.

Local Government

Henry John Millidge, born in 1915, was a Worthing local government clerk, who lived with his parents at 'Ryall', in Uplands Avenue. The house was damaged by a bomb in November 1940 but no-one was killed.

Ernest J. Lidbetter, a retired local government officer, of 'West Ways', Hayling Rise, was secretary of the Poor Law Examination Board.

For many years, the owner and occupier of High Salvington Mill, Walter Douglas-Jones, was a Worthing Corporation councillor. (See a biography in this series, Book One, page 79).

Captain Walter Douglas-Jones.
Photo courtesy of Jean Thomson.

Alfred James Luke OBE, was a member of Worthing Corporation and he represented Durrington Ward. His home was 'Lychgate', at the top of Bost Hill.

In the Register, Joseph Arthur Mason, describes his occupation as company director, his own cycle business, but he was very active in Worthing local government, including being Mayor twice. (See his biography in this series, Book Three, page 38). He lived at 'Throstle Nest', Newling Way.

Municipal clerk, Percy Samms Nichols, of 'Crockendale', Mill Lane, born in Hornsey, worked for the Borough Council, Catford.

Harold James Phillips was Worthing's medical officer of health. (See his biography on page 18). He lived in Honeysuckle Lane at 'The Field House'.

Single occupations

A few occupations are mentioned only once in the 1939 Register. For instance, John Lambourne, of 'Sapintas', Mill Lane, was an agriculturalist which, according to the dictionary, is someone who is an expert on agriculture and who advices farmers. He was on the staff of the Dept of Agriculture in the Straits Settlements and the Federated Malay States.

There are two artists, Georgina Marjorie "Madge" Graham and her sister, Lady Chalmers. (See their biographies on pages 10 and 11).

Musically, there is one piano tuner, Frederick R Mayor, of 'Courtlands', in Salvington Hill, one singer and one cellist.

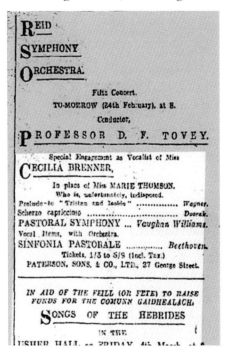

Reid Symphony Orchetra advertisement.
'The Scotsman' 23 February 1927.

The singer, appropriately named Caecilie (Latin, St. Caecilia, was the goddess of musicians) Karoline Brenner but known professionally as plain Cecilia Brenner. She was a soprano from Holland. Born in 1890, she lived much of her life in Britain and in 1928 she applied to the British Home Secretary for naturalisation. She sang in concerts in London, Liverpool and Edinburgh and in February 1927 took the place of Marie Thomson, who was indisposed, singing with the Reid Symphony Orchestra conducted by Professor D. F. Tovey. She could be heard frequently on the radio, also. She must have been particularly fond of High Salvington because in 1939, in retirement, she was living with Rev.and Mrs Greenwood at 'Tudor Lodge', Palmers Way, and when she moved it was only to 'Hertmore Cottage', in Salvington Hill, in the early 1940s and after that to 'Lynhay', Cherry Walk until the early 1960s when she went to 'Cornerways', in Ashacre Lane, Salvington.

The only cellist mentioned in the 1939 Register is Stella B. Fife. She is referred to in Grove's Dictionary of Music as being a member of SWM (Society of Women Musicians), which existed between 1911 and 1920, and she is mentioned in a book by Laura Seddon called " British Women Composers and Instrumental Chamber Music in the early Twentieth Century" published by

BROADCASTING.

—

Home and Foreign Programmes.

—

ABERDEEN (214.3 metres).   From
10.15—Daily Service .... London
10.30—Time Signal .... Do.
10.45—''The Week in Westminster''
    —Major C. R. Attlee, M.P. ... Do.
12.0 —Studio Orchestra and Helen
    Morris (contralto) ....Edinburgh
1.15—Philharmonic Midday Concert—
    Cecilia Brenner (mezzo-sop-
    rano); Friedrich Wuhrer
    (pianoforte) ....Birmingham

Radio broadcast advertisement. 'Aberdeen Press and Journal' 3 Nov 1932.

BERKS TRAINING COLLEGE
OF MUSIC,
AT
17, CROSS STREET, READING.
Director,
MR. WALTER MACFARREN.
Principal,
MISS BEATRICE MURCHISON, L.R.A.M.
Vice Principals,
MISS EVELINE FIFE, L.R.A.M., (Violinist.)
MISS STELLA FIFE. ('Cellist.)
The HALF TERM COMMENCES MONDAY,
FEBRUARY 28th.
For Prospectus, apply to the Secretary.

Berks Training College of Music. 'Reading Mercury' 19 February 1898.

Routledge. Her home was at 'Berry Mount', West Hill. Stella was a pupil of William Whitehouse (1859-1935) English cellist and teacher at the Royal Academy of Music, the Royal College of Music and King's College, Cambridge. Stella Fife and her sister, Eveline, a violinist, were vice-principals of Berks Training College of Music at 17, Cross Street, Reading, which was founded by the principal, Beatrice Murchison L.R.A.M., in May 1897. A director of the College was Walter Cecil MacFarren, (1826-1905) English pianist, composer and conductor and teacher at the Royal Academy of Music. In 1928, the Cobbett Challenge medal, offered for the best performance by a string quartet, was won by a group made up of Effie Armour, Kitty Wilkinson, Kathleen Easton and Stella Fife.

CHAPTER SEVEN

ANDY BARTRAM'S REMINISCENCES

In December 2015, Andy Bartram requested Books One and Two of "A History of High Salvington" and I delivered them to 'High View' hoping to meet him but there was no-one in so I put them through the letter box.

Later that day he e-mailed me sounding enthusiastic about High Salvington, full of interest in the area, eager to share his memories with me and promising to introduce me to a couple of close friends who were also willing to reminisce about their time in High Salvington.

Christmas and New Year came and went and when I contacted him again he said he was still keen to share anecdotes though he would be away until Easter but then he would be in touch. Despite e-mailing him, I did not hear from him again.

Fortunately, his December e-mail was full of interesting details which I quote here in his own words as I am sure he meant me to use the material.

View from the steps of High Salvington Windmill 1919. Francis Frith via Ancestry.

"Since moving into 'High View' in Sept 1992, I have read much about the local area and done my best to discover the history of my house, whose previous owners were Councillor Peter and Christine Searle who owned the Ford garage 'Searles' in Worthing on the current Waitrose site in the centre of Worthing. Within a short time of moving in, I had the pleasure of chatting over the telephone with Christine. They had bought the house at auction in 1956. 'High View' then had the land which is now occupied by 'Silver Birches', 'New Dawn House' and 'The Oaks'. I have the Sale catalogue if you would care to see it at some stage as it outlines who originally owned the land in 1923 when the house was built".

Frankie Vaughan. www.richardedwards.info.

"Also on the Francis Frith Website for old photographs, our house can be seen in the picture taken from the top of the windmill steps. The picture is looking North onto three houses which are in Gorse lane. In the distance, between the second and third house, our house, 'High View' can be seen with its two dormer windows and two chimneys. The houses you can see in the foreground surrounded in Gorse are 'Cissbury Cottage', on the corner of West Hill and Gorse Lane with its neighbouring house 'Tanglewood' and then 'Camelia House 'at the far right of the picture. If you look carefully at the picture, the top of 'Rest Harrow' can just be seen to the right of 'High View'.

"Christine informed me that Frankie Vaughan to spend his summers at 'Rest Harrow' just along the road from me. You mention 'Rest Harrow' in your first book. When I moved here in 1993, the Director of the London & Edinburgh

Semprini. Youtube.com

Insurance Company lived at 'Rest Harrow' and his chauffeur used to collect him each morning in a Jaguar which had the number plate LE3.

"One of our dear friends, Pam, grew up in 'The Vyne' as a child and recalls many stories for us. She remembers attending parties in the grounds of 'Furzeholme' and hearing Semprini play there.

"Another dear friend, John, grew up in a detached house called 'St Avits' which was at the corner of Palmers Way and Salvington Hill. I believe there were three houses in the plot where the Berkley Homes were built in the early 1980's. There is, however, one gate post which remains and can be seen from the junction of Hayling Rise."

The one remaining gatepost.
Photo by the author.

Frank Abelson CBE was born in Liverpool in 1928, the son of Jewish immigrants. He took the stage name of **Vaughan** from his grandmother. Although he really wanted to be a boxer, he began singing with a dance band, entered a radio talent competition in London and his long career in entertainment developed from that. When he died in 1999, he had not totally retired.

Although of Italian descent, **Semprini** (Alberto Fernando Riccardo Semprini) was born in Bath in 1908 and is referred to as an English pianist, composer and conductor. He was well-known for his radio broadcasts – 'Semprini Serenade' was aired for 25 years from 1957. His opening words were "old ones, new ones, loved ones, neglected ones". He died in Brixham in 1990.

CHAPTER EIGHT

High Salvington Residents' Association

Compiled by Mary Meadows

High Salvington Residents' Association (HSRA) was established on 28th October 1970 for the purpose of preventing closure of the Village Shop and development of that site.

The minutes of the first meeting held in the, then, 'Chalet Café', Furze Road read:

"Mr H E Muskett was unanimously elected Chairman and Mr F J Wilkie was elected as Secretary.

It was proposed by Mr Clinch and seconded by Mr Wilkie that a committee be formed to explore the possibilities of purchasing wholly or in part the empty corner shop at the cross roads of Furze Road/Honeysuckle Lane/Salvington Hill. This in order to preserve the characteristics of the premises and its environs.

The following were duly elected to form the committee: -

Mr W Clinch; Miss A Allan; Mr R Curtis; Mr H S Watts; Miss R Charles; Mr R B Henly

It was proposed by Mr H Watts and seconded by Mrs Carter that all such meetings in the future should be known as The High Salvington Residents' Association. Until such time as the aforegoing committee are able to make a report the meeting was duly adjourned.

Planning permission was later refused on the grounds that, "Existing shopping use of the site should be maintained."

By November 1970 membership stood at 24 households. Today, membership consists of 800 households equating to 87% of the households within High Salvington.

Over time the objectives have changed to adapt to differing circumstances. The current HSRA objectives are:

a) *To advance and protect the interests of all resident members, especially in regard to any proposed development plans for the area which are considered detrimental to the ambiance and environmentally adverse to the High Salvington area.*

b) *To promote the provision and improvement of local amenities.*

Philip Povey's retirement - 2010 – having been presented with antique maps of High Salvington by the Committee.

Mary Meadows
Chairman of the HSRA

To date, the late Philip Povey, who joined in 1994, is the longest serving committee member. Philip held the positions of Chairman; Honorary Treasurer; Planning Liaison; Membership Secretary & Newsletter Editor. At times, Philip held multiple roles and in doing so was undoubtedly responsible for the Association's survival. Philip retired in 2010.

Fred Weller became Chairman in 2008, serving until May 2012.

Following Philip's retirement in 2010, Mary Meadows was elected as Membership Secretary & Newsletter Editor. In addition to Mary's aforementioned role, she was then elected Chairman in 2012.

Other HSRA Committee roles, not mentioned above, are those of Honorary Secretary; Emergency Services Liaison; Assistant Membership Secretary & Newsletter Editor; Activities & Events Co-ordinator. All Councillors serving High Salvington also sit as, non-voting, members on the HSRA Committee.

Currently, the A27, for which there is an HSRA project role – 'A27 & Wider Environment', is of top priority. In September 2017, the HSRA rejected Highways England' proposal for junction improvements, which would cost the tax payer £69m and apparently only reduce journey times by between 3 to 5 minutes.

As HSRA is a voluntary organization, praise is therefore due to all committee members, both past and present, for their services to High Salvington.

CHAPTER NINE

FULL CIRCLE

The turbulent life of High Salvington Windmill

Richard Budgen map of 1724. Worthing Reference Library.

Exactly when High Salvington windmill was built is not known but she appears on Richard Budgen's map of **1724** and may have existed before that. The estimated date has varied from 1700 to 1750 but now seems to have settled on **c.1774**.

She (windmills are female – like ships) is a post mill with the main body and its machinery resting on a crown tree which is supported on and rotates round a massive central wooden post which in turn is held a few inches off the ground on a trestle of horizontal cross-bars and diagonal quarter bars.

Originally, she would have had four common sails, (sometimes called 'swifts' in Sussex). Eventually, as now, High Salvington had one pair of common sails and one pair of shutter sails.

The shutter sail, which resembles a venetian blind, was invented by Andrew Meikle, a Scot, in **1772**. Whereas the miller had the lengthy and dangerous job of climbing the ladder-like framework of the common sail in order to cover it with canvas to catch the wind, the shutter sail had a series of louvres that could be opened or closed by levers.

The earliest known miller at High Salvington was Edmund Drewitt. He is credited with being the first in Sussex to insure a mill against fire on 21 January **1775**. At that time the mill was valued at £250. Some accounts say that the insuring company was Sun Fire Office and that their fire mark was above the door and on one of the main beams. Other sources say that the insuring company was Royal Exchange and the policy no. was 33161. Both claims sound plausible and are both correct. A business was established by Charles Povey in London in 1708 called the Royal Exchange Fire Office which moved to an office near the Royal Exchange and became the Sun Fire Office in 1710. It is the oldest fire insurance company still in existence – known from 1996 as the Royal and Sun Alliance.

Andrew Meikle. Portrait by A. Reddock. www.en.wikipedia.org

The names and dates of other known millers are:

William Sheppard **1792**

John Harwood **1839**

Daniel Redman **1824 – 1843**

William Day Beard **1847 – 1862**

John Sheppard **1849**

Thomas Hampton **c.1850**

Charles Davey **1863 – 1865**

Walter West **1865 – 1869**

Emily Beard, widow of William Day Beard **1869**

Henry Ball, assistant miller **1872**

Emily Beard 1874, assisted by Henry Ball, journeyman miller

Henry Ball **1875 -1876**

William Brown **1869 -1897**

William Day Beard lived at Salvington Cottage, West Tarring and in the 1861 census he is described as a 'Master Miller employing two men', presumably John Sheppard and Thomas Hampton, which would explain the overlap of dates. He died on 4 July 1862, aged only 42. Millers, like coalminers, often suffered respiratory illnesses. Years of breathing flour dust was as damaging as breathing coal dust. The death certificate states that he died of "Chronic Bronchitis Ulceration of Trachea and Bronchial Vessels." The added words "about 18 months" convey a great deal of suffering.

The mill is generally quoted as having ceased working in **1897** but there are references to Alfred Coote, a baker, using her in **1898**, to Thomas Coote & Sons (presumably the same family) making improvements and using her in **1914** and of George Brown even later than that.

In **1906**, the mill and a considerable amount of surrounding land, was bought by Alfred Charles Jackson. He removed the wooden roundhouse that enclosed the trestle in **1907** and replaced it with an octagonal cast concrete roundhouse with large sash windows. Soon Salvington Mill Tea Rooms were being advertised and Fletcher Cole is recorded as running a refreshment room at the site and a Miss Cole was proprietress.

Salvington Mill c.1890.

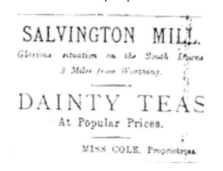

Advertisement for Salvington Mill teas. Worthing Gazette 2 October 1907.

A survey of all properties in the country was carried out under the Finance (1909-1910) Act – similar to the Domesday survey of 1086. Each property was given a number which was entered in a Field Book by the district valuer. The High Salvington mill site number was 7684 and the valuer paid his visit during September **1913**. In his small handwriting he gave the following description of what he saw.

"Property consists of an old Windmill, which has been repaired and there has been erected at foot a one storey wooden building now used as a tea-room. This building is well built and some underpinning was I understand necessary before it could be built.

"There is an old Cottage, built of bk (brick) and partly of timber containing 3 rooms K (kitchen) Sc (scullery) 2 ? E.Cs (earth closets). Water tank underground cost about £20.

"A newer building is a one-story cottage 'The Retreat' containing one room, small kitchen and large verandah in front.

"There are altogether 3 tanks on the property and a cesspool. Together with this property goes the right to use the road to the Mill from Salvington (A valuable right in Jackson's view)."

In pencil was added "Mr Jackson roughly estimates outlay of £700 but he has not kept an accurate record."

There seems to be a discrepancy in the records between the concrete roundhouse being built in **1907** and the wooden building "at foot" in **1913**. Perhaps "at foot" meant close beside the mill rather than beneath it because if it had been beneath the mill it could not have been other than one storey.

High Salvington Mill's 150th birthday was celebrated in **1924** and a cake was baked specially for the ocassion.

Some accounts say that the mill was bought by Captain Walter Douglas-Jones in 1925 but his name does not appear in Directories before **1928**. He and his wife, Mary MacDonald Douglas-Jones lived in Mill Cottage until **1957** and ran the tea-rooms during the summer months.

The Windmill House Agency was also based on the site in the **1920s**. Their advertisement read:

"HIGH SALVINGTON Four miles from Worthing 400ft above sea level. Glorious views of Downs and Sea. If you wish to Buy a House or sell one furnished come to the Agents on the spot who have the keys and will personally conduct you over all the available properties in the district – THE WINDMILL HOUSE AGENCY at the OLD WINDMILL."

'Salvington Mill and Tea Rooms' 1910. Worthing Library postcard.

Cake for the Mill's 120th birthday in 1924. Guide to the Windmill 1928.

A storm damaged the mill at the end of **1927**. Heavy rain had fallen on Christmas Day and Boxing Day then the temperature had plummeted and there was a blizzard during which the top of one of the sails broke off.

More damaged was caused in **1929**. A postcard dated 15 April (though not with a picture of the mill) had the message "Salvington windmill lost one of its sails last November and it looks very odd indeed now." The remaining sails were shortened to prevent further damage.

The Mill in the snow – note the damaged sail. Worthing Herald 31 December 1927.

Christopher Wenlock, who wrote an article entitled "The Restored Mills of Sussex" in the August **1938** issue of the Sussex County Magazine, stated that the mill had been thoroughly restored and for a small fee visitors could inspect the machinery which was in perfect working order. He pointed out that High Salvington Mill was possibly the only one to be used as a tea-room.

High Salvington Mill, 27 August 1939.
Lawrie Dean Collection no 152.

It is probably not strictly true that the mill was "fully restored" or "in perfect working order" but, more likely, been repaired to look attractive to visitors.

On 11 October **1949** the windmill was surveyed as a listed building. She was registered as being in Furze Road at the map reference TQ 10NW 23/69. The report stated that the former

Durrington Mill was the post type with a modernised roundhouse, that it had tarred timbers,that its machinery was in working order, that here was a fan tail and that the date 1700 appeared over the door. Only 3 sails were intact.

West Sussex County Council prepared a report in **1954** which proposed the preservation of an example of each type of mill in Sussex. Shipley was to represent the smock type, Halnaker the tower type, West Ashling the rare combination of wind and water type and High Salvington the post type as it was the last remaining example.

The Mill in August 1952.
Mills Archive - Guy Blytheman.

In **July 1954**, High Salvington mill was the subject of a report prepared by county council planning officers with guidance from D. W. Muggeridge, deputy clerk of Worthing District Council, and Rex Walles – both described as windmill experts. The result was a document which still maintained that the mill's central post was a living oak rooted in the ground and that she was in a good state of repair, despite missing one of her sails. She was already scheduled as an ancient monument and it was thought that it would need little spent on her to restore her to first class condition. Capt. Douglas-Jones wanted to sell. Other counties, including Kent, Surrey, Essex, East Suffolk and Yorkshire, were engaged in similar projects.

A detailed description of High Salvington Mill appeared in the Worthing Gazette early in **1955** in an article by Henfrey Smail. He wrote "Salvington Mill is actually in the parish of Durrington and in the early records is referred to as Durrington Mill.

"The present brick roundhouse, now used as a tea-room, is a modern structure built about 1900 to replace the original roundhouse."

His reference to a brick roundhouse not a concrete one is interesting. Perhaps he wrote his article without visiting the place, taking his material from the writings of others. The High Salvington Mill Trust took down the concrete structure and re-instated the wooden roundhouse during restoration. They know the mill intimately, having taken her apart and reassembled her, so I believe that it was a concrete building.

Inside one of the tea pavilions. Guide to the Windmill 1949.

A tea pavilion, derelict. 'Mill Cottage' behind.

Two ladies taking tea. 1930s. 'Mill Cottage' in the background. Terry Childs Collection. TC0980.

A room inside 'Mill Cottage'. Photo by Alex Low 1964.

The Gazette article goes on "Early views of the mill show the graceful cut of the skirt, or tower edge of the mill body, which is curved to clear the roundhouse roof. This suggests that the old wooden roundhouse and the mill itself were more probably contemporary. Usually, if a post mill started life without a roundhouse as many very early mills did, the lower edge of the body was cut straight.

"The mill contains two pairs of stones, one Peak and one Burr, which bear the makers' tablet, Coombe & Co., 30, Mark Lane, London.

"The machinery includes a grader, or wire machine, consisting of a wire gauze drum which was used for cleaning and grading the flour, and a friction driven hoist for raising or lowering the sacks. The mill also possesses a complete set of dresser's tools, for re-dressing the stones when they become worn."

Henfrey Smail, comparing High Salvington Mill with Broadwater Mill observed that she had been better cared for. Broadwater Mill was due for demolition but because Capt. and Mrs Douglas-Jones had lived at Mill Cottage on site and had made repairs in order to use the mill as a visitor attraction, it had withstood the passage of time more robustly.

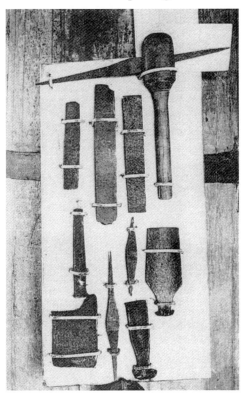

Stone dressers tools used at the Mill.
West Sussex Record Office PH 11214.

Henfrey Smail mentions the damage caused in the 'great storm' of Christmas **1927** "when one of the sails was smashed and part of the weatherboarding stripped from the body. As a temporary measure the broken sail was removed entirely, leaving only the whip, and the others were shortened. In **1935** the bodywork was again repaired and parts of the timber framework were strengthened with iron straps."

He ended his article with reference to the recommendation of the County Planning Committee that Worthing Corporation should purchase the mill and put in hand immediate repairs so as to be "assured of preservation."

What to do about the mill was still being discussed. The Worthing Gazette in **1955** reported that councillors were concerned about the rise in the estimated cost of repair. Alderman F. J. Nash recalled that when repair was first considered the figure was £300. That had soon become £1,500 and now it was £1,800. No-one liked to see the disappearance of these windmills but was preservation practicable, he wondered?

Councillor F. Kenton added that the cost of £1,800 was neither finite nor binding on the people concerned but, in general, they were all in favour of saving the mill. As the Ministry of Works had marked her as an ancient monument, she could not be knocked down.

Councillor H. D. Steele, who lived at 'Kinfauns', High Salvington, agreed that the council should retain the mill. He was surprised by the number of times they dithered over this issue. The mill was a fine landmark and would eventually become a fine amenity and possibly a very profitable one. It was part of Sussex and part of Worthing. Much was spent

Horace D Steele.
Drawn by the author.

on the seafront but, in his opinion, the beauties of Worthing were in the country round about.

The Windmill during repair August 1960.
Mills Archive- Kenneth C. Ferrier.

Councillor A. J. Barrett, too, was amazed that further discussion was taking place as a decision had been made by the General Purposes Committee months ago and the Town Clerk had been given authority to negotiate. E. G. Townsend, OBE, agreed that he had consulted the district valuer and had made an offer to purchase the mill but it had been refused.

Alderman T. A. Clifford, aware of the time factor, pointed out that the building was being attacked by worm and possibly beetle. If left it would rapidly become unrepairable. At this moment, however, it could be preserved.

The Finance Committee recommended that the Borough Engineer should carry out repairs at the cost of £1,800.

The difference of opinion seemed to be over whether or not the building should be repaired while still in private ownership. Alderman Clifford, chairman of the Finance and Law Committee, asked for clarification of the situation.

E. G. Townsend, OBE, Town Clerk, explained that formerly it had been the plan to preserve the mill in private ownership but now it was thought that a better course of action would be to buy outright.

The Finance and Law Committee agreed that if the property was improved and purchased later the value would have risen and it would have to be bought at a higher price.

The Town Clerk was asked to negotiate further with the owners for an option to buy on vacation by the present life tenant, at a price fixed by the district valuer.

A drawing of the Mill by Barbara Russon. West Sussex Gazette 24 January 1957.

Nothing seems to have happened for about 5 years but Worthing Borough Council eventually bought the mill in **1959** from Mrs Douglas-Jones, whose husband had died on 2 December 1957, for £2,250 on the condition that she could continue to live at Mill Cottage, for a nominal rent.

In **1959**, also, the High Salvington Windmill Trust was set up. It consisted of representatives from the Weald and Downland Open Air Museum at Singleton, near Chichester, Worthing Borough Council and the Friends of Salvington Mill.

J. T. Mackley & Co. Ltd., of Small Dole, were employed to hoist the buck two feet clear of the mill post so that repair and replacement could be completed. The cost of this manoeuvre alone was £6,000.

Further work was undertaken by the West Sussex Rural Engineering Co. of Earnley, near Bognor. The Mill Trust with only £15,000 at their disposal appealed for more funds.

In the spring of **1960** Edwin Hole, millwrights of Burgess Hill, were given until the autumn to complete immediate repairs but they found that the structure was in a worse state than had been thought. As much would be preserved as possible but some timbers were "liable to crumble off in the hand." At this point the mill was at her lowest ebb.

She was sagging because two of the four main cross timbers were broken and more than half of the framework was ravaged by death watch beetle. G. H. Kempton, the Borough Engineer, said, "We knew that much of the mill was rotten but not that there was any beetle." The timbers that were left in place were treated with insecticide and strengthened with wooden and steel brackets and plates.

The floor of the roundhouse was found to be severely damaged by dry rot and was replaced with concrete. New steps and new common sails ('dead' or decorative, not functional) were fitted and new weatherboarding was applied. This work, originally estimated to cost £350 and expected to be finished towards the end of **1960**, eventually cost £4,983 and took until the summer of **1961**.

Despite the improved appearance of the mill, visitors complained that there were not enough facilities. However, when the Town Council responded by proposing that private enterprise should build a café and a large car park, 106 local residents signed a petition saying that "it would result in the commercialisation of an essentially residential and rural neighbourhood, and would spoil the special charm and character of the area."

The Entertainment Committee compromised with a plan to provide parking for 6 cars adjacent to Furze Road at a cost of £30 and they recommended spending £3,700 on building a bungalow to be let out at £6 13s, excluding rates, to a caretaker who would supervise the mill. He would be expected to maintain the grounds at his own expense (it cost the Corporation £40 – £50 a year for grass cutting) and be available from May to September to show visitors round.

The Corporation would receive 25% of the admission receipts. None of these proposals seem to have been carried out.

In short, the existence of the mill hung in the balance – she had only been given palliative care and was still vulnerable.

In **August 1971**, 15-year-old Sarah-Jane Holmes, of 638, Birmingham Road, Lydiate Ash, Bromsgrove, Worcestershire, visited the mill and was appalled. She and a friend obtained the keys from "a nearby family" and they found the mill floor covered in "broken pieces of wood" and "a complete mess". "The upper storey was in an equal amount of mess", she said, " Separate pieces of machinery were all over the floor and hardly anything was in complete working order."

She concluded, "I find it very hard to understand why a place which is interesting, a landmark, and of such historical value, should be allowed to deteriorate in such a way." She endorsed the suggestion that a small property might be bought to house a couple to look after the mill and that a charge should be made to cover expenses to those wishing to visit it.

Worthing's deputy borough architect, R. Horswell, responded with the comment, "I think this young lady was expecting to find much more there than we provide. It is not a working mill at all. The machinery she mentions is, in fact, mill machinery laid out on the floor for display." He explained that the mill was inspected twice a year to determine what repairs and maintenance were necessary, and provision was made in the estimate for these items. The sails were moved round once a year to prevent warping.

Mr Horswell also said that it would be too costly to build a property for a caretaker and, anyway, the couple who held the keys reported any matters that needed attention. To give him his due, he went to see the mill for himself and said that he found some small pieces of worm-eaten wood that had collapsed on to the floor.

A noticeboard was put up in **1975** with a few historical details and three council departments were supposed to look after the mill. Maintenance was the responsibility of the architect's department, viewing and access were in the hands of the amenities department and the surrounding ground was one of the duties of the engineer's department. The sails were turned a quarter revolution once a year to prevent "sag and distortion."

By **1976** the derelict state of the mill had become much more widely known. Berenice Mitchell, who lived at Mill Lodge, 9, Furze Road, sent a letter to the Herald. "I have numerous callers," she wrote, "among them tourists from abroad, asking for details of its history and if there is literature available. Many are dismayed at the condition into which it has fallen." She invited people to contact her "to discuss a plan of campaign."

In the same issue of the Gazette, Mrs G. A. Clayden, of 37, Salvington Hill, wrote "I was staggered to read that High Salvington windmill is such a bad state". She suggested a museum in the roundhouse and a kiosk where one could buy a cup of tea and a sandwich. She mentioned the Mayor's suggestion that Worthing Civic Society might help. She wondered also if the Friends of Worthing Museum, the Archaeological Society and the Historical Society could offer help. "Once it collapses it has gone forever", she warned and pointed out "A penny from every household would go a long way to help the sails keep turning."

Councillor Thomas Ayscough, for his part, thought that "If it had been worthy of repair it would have been done by now. The roof leaks, the centre pivot has death watch beetle – like me, it's a wreck – and I do not think we should do anything about it."

Whether or not this was the prevailing opinion of Worthing Town Council they were reported as not being able to afford the estimated £20,000 needed for repair, let alone restoration.

The Mill in a desperate state. 1979.

Martin Brunnarius, in his book "Windmills of Sussex", published in **1979**, wrote "When visiting here on one of the open days I found the spout floor empty except for a pair of sack scales and a stone governor resting on the floor. Above in the stone floor, the first thing noticed is the little window in the breast which looks out over the canister end of the windshaft. The view is out over Worthing from this hill, 300ft or so

The old crown tree with the date 1774 carved into it. Worthing Herald July 1984.

above the sea. We find here that the brakewheel has gone, removed several years ago because of infestation with woodworm and death watch beetle, two of the many deadly enemies of the windmill. The tail wheel remains, as does a pair of French burrs in the tail of the mill with its iron 'horse frame' and the peaks in the head. It is hoped that these and the remaining machinery will be restored to a working condition in the not-too-distant future,"

"An inspection of the structure had revealed that she is badly weakened by rot and beetle, and now lists a little to the west. Sad to say, she is an unhappy site (sic) standing in long grass and surrounded by a safety fence."

The Mill still ailing but open to the public. August 1981. Photo by Frank Gregory.

At some point in the **1970s** gale force winds apparently left the mill without sails at all and she remained in that state at least until **1980**, according to "Sussex Life". Even in that condition, the same article described Salvington Mill as the finest example of a post mill still existing in Sussex.

In October **1980**, steel scaffolding was erected to support the main body of the mill while the trestle was replaced. At last, restoration had begun, rather than repair and patching up.

In **1981** the crown post, which now lies on the ground beside the gatehouse, was removed. The date 1774 was carved into it but it has now weathered away. A new crown post was made and put into place and on **28 July 1983** the mill could turn once more. Flooring was renewed and the mill stones put back. Progress had been made but many more years of work remained at a cost of between £10,000 and £20,000.

Felipe Edwards, chairman of the Friends of High Salvington, said that the cladding (weatherboarding), wooden gearing and the sails needed to be repaired. Throughout the restoration process the mill was regularly opened to the public during the summer and many fund-raising events were organised. The first Open Day was held in **1981** and the first Summer Fete in **1982**.

Patrick Moore at the Summer Fete. 1984. Worthing Herald.

The Fete held in July **1984** raised £1,000 and was attended by 1,500 visitors. A guest on that day was Patrick Moore, the astronomer, well-known for 'The Sky at Night' BBC television programme. Also present was Worthing's Town Crier of the time, Philip Holliday.

The West Hedge was planted in **1985** with a mixture of hawthorn, blackthorn and maple.

New sails were in place by **May 1988** and were fully functional. A huge achievement. Another great step forward was the reconstruction of the wooden roundhouse, costing £40,000 and completed in the spring of **1990**.

High Salvington Windmill finally came fully to life on **4 April 1991** when 50lbs of flour was ground.

A **Granary** was viewed by the Trust at Tickeridge Farm, near Kingscote, close to the Bluebell Railway in 1993. It took a year for the owners to agree a sale but in **June 1994** the fragile structure was conveyed to the site, restored and re-erected. One of the steddle stones it stands on had to be replaced and was made from the same seam of sandstone as the others at Philpotts' Quarry, near West Hoathly.

The **New Barn** was built in **1997/98** during the winter and often by floodlights in the evenings. The actual building cost £147, covered by a grant. Fixtures and fittings were extra for which funds had to be raised. The completed building received a Distinction in Building award from Worthing Borough Council in **1998**. Now, there were kitchen facilities and flush toilets on the site.

The Gatehouse. Photo by the author 2014.

The green bench formerly at Ford Station. Photo by the author 2017.

The Nutley wind generator. Photo by the author 2017.

The Glynde wind pump. Photo by the author 2017.

Inside the concrete roundhouse, 1977. Photo by Frank Gregory.

Inside the concrete roundhouse when it was a tea room. The postcard is postmarked November 1916.
On the counter to the right 'Fry's Sweet Chocolate' is advertised. Pinned to the central post is a notce saying
'NO SMOKING Allowed' and another saying 'Admission to upper part of mill 2d'. Colin Clissold collection
CC1806.

The Granary. Photo by the author 2017.

The West Hedge was mature enough to be layered. The Green Bench, acquired from Ford station in 1980 was finally restored in **2012** painted railway green.

With the essential restoration virtually complete, ironically, volunteer numbers fell. So alarmingly, in fact, it was feared that the Summer Fete, the biggest fund-raiser of the mill's year, might have to be cancelled as there were too few people to run it. However, at a meeting held in **January 2012**, fifty new volunteers came forward and literally saved the day.

At the end of the following year the mill, now a Grade II listed building, featured in an episode of "Tudor Monastery Farm", one of the 'Farm' series presented by Ruth Goodman, Peter Ginn, Alex Langlands and Tom Penfold. The episode was first shown by BBC2 on Wednesday 27 November **2013**.

A new set of steps were made in **2016**. Fifteen men hauled them from the building site to the mill where they were hoisted into position by rope and pulley.

High Salvington Windmill was not free of problems even now, however. They were not the structural kind this time but those caused by the surrounding trees and buildings which threatened to prevent the wind reaching her sails. Building applications, including a garage, in **2016** that threatened to raise the height of properties near the mill were concerning the Trust and the Friends.

It was hoped that protection of the windmill would be part of the new Worthing local plan which would set out areas suitable for development until 2033 and that "developers would be required to submit their own wind studies to demonstrate their plans would not negatively impact on the mill's operation." There were only two wind directions remaining – from the south west and the north east.

Tom Wye, former Mayor of Worthing, chairman of the High Salvington Mill Trust and mill guide, was concerned that "If any new development was permitted in these areas the mill would be unable to operate."

A government inspector disagreed. He said "Building Research Establishment work on wind engineering suggests that it is generally considered that the effect of a building only extends for four times its height. In this instance, given the height of the garage and the distance from the mill at over about 40 metres, the indication is that the operation of the mill is not affected,"

At the time of writing, this controversy has not been resolved. A Worthing Herald report stated that "the council will now consult with the likes of Historic England and the Sussex Mills Group and consider commissioning a technical study on the issue."

Besides the mill, there are two other interesting structures in the mill field. **The Glynde wind pump**, a hollow-post wind pump, which spent its working life pumping water out of limekilns near Glynde railway station. It ceased working in 1928 and was removed in 1988. It was bought by the High Salvington Mill Trust in **2006** and had been fully restored by **2008**. The original pump engine was lost but has been replaced by a Dando diaphragm pump from a farm in Horsham and it can be seen in action on Open Days.

The second structure is the **Nutley wind engine**, which pumped water for Woodcocks Farm in Nutley, East Sussex. The 18-vane fanwheel is mounted on a tower and it was working until the 1940s when the farm was connected to the mains water supply. It was dismantled in the early 1960s and converted to generate electricity. In the 1980s it was moved to Down Street in Nutley but could not be re-erected as planning permission was refused. The High Salvington Mill Trust acquired it in **2013** and expect to have it working in **2017**.

A bag of flour, ground at the Mill, and a jar of homemade damson jam both bought at the Summer Fete 2017. photo by the author 2017.

For someone who reads a lot of local history and finds that far-too-frequent word "demolished" deeply depressing, the restoration of High Salvington Windmill is a tonic to the soul.

This magnificent building is now as strong as, or perhaps stronger than, the day she was constructed. No praise is too great for the work done by the volunteers who for upwards of twenty years have devoted their time, often over the winter months, to steadfastly working towards the goal of complete restoration.

Although they had the help of machinery, a good deal of human muscle power was also needed to manoeuvre heavy components into and within the mill's confined space.

Over the same period, the money that the mill's visitors spent during all the Open Days and other events at the site was vital in supporting the work being done. At the time of writing it costs £3,000 a year to maintain the mill and it is the visitors that provide this lifeblood. Hopefully, she now has a secure future.

High Salvington Windmill – "Restored to Life". Photo by the author 2014.

APPENDIX ONE

INDEX OF PEOPLE AND PLACES

APPENDIX TWO

Sources of Information

CHAPTER ONE – Biographies

George Herbert Bloye

Worthing Herald 14 February 1931 p11

Worthing Gazette 15 May 1927 p6

11 February 1931 p8

2 December 1931 p7

Ancestry.co.uk

H.J.T. Brackley

Worthing Herald 14 July 1967

England Census 1911

Ancestry.co.uk

Worthing Voters' Lists, Worthing Reference Library

Worthing Gazette 14 April 1965 p13

Elizabeth Graham

Worthing Gazette 2 February 1949

5 December 1951

Worthing Herald 7 December 1951

Ancestry.co.uk

Findmypast.co.uk

Georgina Margaret Graham

Worthing Herald 13 April 1962 p13

Worthing Gazette 2 February 1949 p5

Reply from 'Punch' July 2017

Worthing Voters' Lists, Worthing Reference Library

Sir William George Maxwell

Kelly's Directory 1938

1939 Register

Findmypast.co.uk

Ancestry.co.uk

'Who's Who in Worthing and District' 1928/29

httpps://db.ipohworld.org

https://rvisva.files.worldpress.com viewed 24 November 2016

Worthing Herald 28 August 1959

https://sembangkuala.wordpress.com viewed 24 November 2016

Hendon and Finchley Times 29 August 1902

Portsmouth Evening News 13 January 1883

British Knights of the Realm Index Transcription

National Probate Calendar (Index of Wills)

England census 1881

https://www.globalsecurity.org (Malaysia history) viewed 27 November 2016

https://en.wikipedia.org/wiki/George Maxwell viewed 27 November 2016

Reginald Arthur Mitchell

A Millenium Encyclopedia of Worthing History by D. R. Elleray 1998

Kelly's Directories for Worthing

Worthing Gazette 12 January 1977 front page

Worthing Herald 14 January p40

Worthing Voters' Lists

England Census 1911

Dr Harold James Phillips

Worthing Herald 8 June 1945

Census of Ireland 1911

Ancestry.co.uk

Findmypast.co.uk

CHAPTER TWO – Tunnel Tragedy

Worthing Herald 10 February 1937 front page

Worthing Gazette 13 February 1937

CHAPTER THREE – The Housekeeper's Story

Worthing Gazette 11 February 1931 p8

Worthing Herald 14 February 1931

Ancestry.co.uk

https://en.wikipedia.org

CHAPTER FOUR – Tudor Lodge Children's Hotel

Worthing Herald 20 April 1956 front page, pp9 and 14

Kelly's Directories for Worthing 1950s

Worthing Voters' Lists

Ancestry.co.uk

Findmypast.co.uk

CHAPTER FIVE – Nutshells

Sources quoted within the chapter

CHAPTER SIX – High Salvington in 1939

en.wikipedia.org

1939 Register via Findmypast.co.uk

Postcard Collections, Worthing Library

Worthing Gazette

National Maritime Museum

West Sussex Record Office, Chichester

Ancestry.co.uk

Kelly's Directories

Mary Steel

Jean Thomson

Newspapers via Findmypast.co.uk

CHAPTER SEVEN – Andy Bartram's Reminiscences

Information in an e-mail from Mr. Bartram

Google images

CHAPTER EIGHT – High Salvington Residents' Association

written by Mary Meadows

CHAPTER NINE – Full Circle

'High Salvington Mill' (DVD) Restoration 1976-1992 and a year in the life of the mill

'The Mill Field Story', High Salvington Mill Trust Ltd 2013

'Salvington Mill' by John Norton Worthing Museum and Art Gallery 1990

'High Salvington Windmill' leaflet, High Salvington Mill Trust late 1990s

'The Mill' newsletter of the Friends of High Salvington Windmill, various dates

'High Salvington Windmill' booklet, reprint 1949

'The Saving of Salvington Mill' Sussex Life November 1980 pp50-51

Post Office Directories

Worthing Voters' Lists

Worthing Herald

Worthing Gazette

'Introduction to the History of Durrington' yellow-covered file, Worthing Reference Library

The Mills Archive https://millsarchive.org

Walkers Quarterly 'Windmills of Sussex' by G. M. Fowell 1930 The Keep ESRO

'Around Historic Sussex' by Ray Miller. 1971 Drawings by Gerald Lip WSRO

Ancestry.co.uk

'Windmills of Sussex' by Martin Brunnarius 1979 Phillimore

'England of the Windmills' by S. P. B. Mais 1931 Dent

'English Windmills' by M. I. Batten 1930

'Windmills in Sussex' by Arthur C. Smith 1971

'Restored Mills of Sussex' by Christopher Wenlock Sussex County Magazine 1938

www. sussexmillsgroup.org.uk

The Sphere 28 August 1954 via Findmypast newspaper collection

Sussex Daily News 30 July 1954